THE

POCKET LIBRARY OF LETTERS

FOR REAL ESTATE PROFESSIONALS

200 Impacting
Model Letters

COMPILED BY
ERNIE BLOOD

Copyright 1991
Carmel Publishing Co., Inc.

Published by Carmel Publishing Co., Inc.
4501 Hills & Dales Road
Canton, Ohio 44718
1-800-344-3834

Carmel Publishing Co., Inc.
4501 Hills & Dales Road, N.W.
Canton, OH 44718

ACKNOWLEDGMENTS

A "Special Thanks" to Karen Hough for all her effort taking this book from an idea to a reality and to all the brokers, managers, secretaries, and sales associates who helped make this book possible by sending in their best letters. Although we were not able to use all of them, we selected the ones that we felt would accomplish the objective of providing the right letter for the right need. We hope the following sample letters can help you with your "Prospects for Success!" If you have a favorite letter that has worked for you and would like to share with our readers, send in a copy in. If it is selected, it will appear in our yearly Library of Letters update.

Contents

FORWARD
by Ernie Blood

Communication, both written and verbal, is the heartbeat of any business. However, when it comes to writing, the most important things seem to be the most difficult to convey into words. Leaving an effective paper trail with potential clients and current customers is essential today and adds credibility to your professional career. The art of communication is not an innate talent. It can and should be cultivated. But where does it all begin?

How does one learn this art of written communication, that is so important to today's business world? For me, in my twenty years of business experience having to communicate with thousands of customers and clients, it was having a "teachable spirit". A willingness to learn from others. When a need arose, I would just ask those who were more talented than I and the answer was provided. As a trainer, having done over 4,000 seminars over the past twenty years, one of the most common questions from students is "How do I communicate with my prospects? What do I say and when do I say it?" Isn't it true that the most important things are always the most difficult to put into words?

It was with this "need to communicate" that the Library of Letters was written. The following letters have been compiled from talented brokers and Realtors throughout the U.S. and Canada in an effort to help you better serve your "Prospects for Success" in saying . . . I would like to be of service, let me introduce myself, thank you, and congratulations. Communication, whether written or verbal, must be practiced and continually improved. These letters should serve as an inspiration for you, but for them to communicate effectively, you must incorporate your own sentiments, ideas and words.

The following letters are "tabbed" for your reference and convenience. The index of letters is provided on the inside of the "tab" for the section you wish to use. Should you have any ideas on good letter writing or a favorite letter you would like to share, please forward them to Carmel Publishing Co., 4501 Hills & Dales Road, N.W., Canton, Ohio 44718 c/o Karen Hough.

Now Let's Communicate

By Bernie Torrence

Communication, what a word! The ability to transmit an idea, a thought or a motive from one person to another. So much has been written of late regarding the art of communication. However, I'm convinced that communication is neither an art nor a science, but a **skill** that can be developed. Have you ever considered that we in America control the world with 26 letters and 10 digits. I've learned that the process of communicating is basically sending and receiving images. We think in images. Imagination is really "Image-ination." Of course the real challenge is to send accurate images to others, as well as to receive accurate images from them, to convey things **exactly** as you see them and to receive them **exactly** as others see them.

In the Real Estate business we are "Word Merchants." We're paid not for the effort of our hand but our communication ability. In today's Real Estate Market it has been found that most buyers and sellers go through 6 months of **pre-decision - indecision** and after they've decided to buy or sell they go through 3 months of **post decision - depression**. As a professional today you are forced to be the communication link in this high emotion time. The business of real estate is simple, but not easy, as is the art of communication.

7

This entire book has been dedicated to the power of words. Mark Twain once said "A powerful agent is the right word, and when we come upon one of these intensely right words the effect is spiritual as well as physical, and electrically prompt." We have chosen words which have worked effectively for many sales people, however, words alone are not the answer. It is the **spirit** in which they are communicated.

A communicator is a leader, you are leading people into a correct decision. As a communicator you must decide on your objective. If you want things to happen, then you must stimulate your clients, either mentally or physically, by applying common sense and logic. Your objective is to get your client to **do** something. Communication is the difference between going on vacation with a road map or leaving it home. **Effective communication is a plan.**

One of the major situations that I've noticed during my 20 years in the sales profession, is that so often we rely on our sales pitch for our listing or sales presentation to do the work for us. Keep in mind that buyers and sellers are people before they are anything else, and they are going to ask themselves continually "What is in this for me?" Before ever giving a presentation or utilizing these words, ask yourself these questions:

1. *How educated is my buyer or seller about the information that I'm going to give them?*
2. *Are they really interested in what I have to say?*
3. *How deep is their level of understanding? Should I adjust my vocabulary to meet their understanding level?*
4. *Do they have strong attitudes about what I'm saying?*
5. *What are their real needs?*
6. *How open minded are they?*
7. *What makes these people special?*
8. *What benefits can I offer them?*

The last two questions . . . how powerful. What **is** special about this client? It was once said that people don't care how much you know until they know how much you care. Every life and family is special, and what they are really looking for is **benefits**. Benefits that can change their lifestyle or thought life, and as a communicator if you are **genuine, enthused** and **professional** enough to choose the right word, you will be able to move the world.

Abraham Lincoln once said "tact is the ability to see others as they see themselves." As a communicator, you must convince me that you believe what you are saying before I can even entertain the thought that I might want to believe what you believe. Keep in mind that you represent knowledge, integrity, solidity, a firm business foundation and that your primary goal is to represent either a seller or a buyer. You've got to believe in what you're doing and you've got to be **credible.** To be credible you must be **truthful**. Keep in mind communication is the art of persuasion, not the art of lying.

You must have **conviction**, your belief can't be weak, it can't be mumbled. **You** have to be excited about **what you** believe.

You must have enthusiasm. That excitement that twinkles in your eyes when you tell somebody what you believe. It's like a fire that spreads and gets other people excited. Keep in mind you are building a relationship, a **client-communicator** relationship. This relationship exists throughout your sales transaction. A national study was done which uncovered this startling fact - **75% of the people who buy or sell real estate never hear from their agent after they bought or sold**, what a shame. We are professionals, let's learn what doctors are learning, about how to relate to patients so that their philosophies and practices can be effectively presented. Recently the medical profession has learned this: "TO ATTRACT AND KEEP PATIENTS, WE MUST TREAT THEM LIKE PEOPLE!" At a recent AMA convention these questions were asked, and what a set of questions they are.

1. How do you see your patients? As a sales agent ask yourself how accessible am I? How committed am I? Is the end result of my presentation to take a listing and run, to rely on the mechanics of our industry to market homes, or am I seeing the big picture and that my ultimate success will be my clients recommending me to their friends.

2. Do we speak the same language? Doctors have learned that it's very difficult to communicate when there's a language barrier. In the real estate profession today, there is a tremendous amount of "shop talk." Be careful that when you utilize words that they are understandable to your client. Make sure you communicate effectively the turnaround time in the current real estate market, so that they can make effective plans for their time.

3. How do we come across with our clients? I have observed in my contact with the real estate industry, both as a professional and as a buyer or seller, that my relationship goes through **3 phases**. The first is when I **like** a person, I may like them because of a recommendation of a friend or the way they look, or how they remind me of someone else, but that's a very shallow basis for a relationship. The next step is when I learn to **respect their knowledge**. This is where they've earned the right to really represent me and it thrusts me into the third phase of our relationship, and that is one of **trust**. I'm convinced that the multi-million dollar producers in today's real estate market are the ones that have moved into a **trust**

relationship with their clients, not by just telling people what they wanted to hear but by telling their clients what was truthful and honest, by handing tough in a hot market and by never apologizing for the marketplace itself.

Yes, we are word merchants, we sell words packaged as ideas. Packaged in a certain way, words become tools of our trade to communicate images, ideas and beliefs. Yes, communication is a skill, not just of actions, but of reactions, so you can react and overrule thought and objections.

Imagine right now that you are holding in your hand a treasure box of great phrases and words that, when spoken or written from the heart, will never fail to gain credibility in your client's mind.

HOW TO USE

USE

THE
POCKET
LIBRARY
OF
LETTERS

HOW TO USE . . .

The Pocket Library of Letters has been created to help you better serve your prospects and clients.

We have divided the book into ten tabs for finger tip reference. Written on the back side of each tab is the index for that section.

Let each letter be a sample to guide you in your prospecting efforts, follow up or follow through. Effective communication is the key to customer satisfaction and repeat business. Remember every prospect, if followed through with, becomes a customer on the average of every 4.8 years. Communication not only makes happy prospects, it makes good dollars and sense.

You now hold in your hand a most important key to your success. It is only by using it, that it can <u>start</u> you in the right direction.

"Happy Letter Writing"

Date

Name
Address
City, State, Zip

Dear _____,

Specializing in condominium living, we are
pleased to present the following special properties:

      1243 Main St. #125 - $199,000
      1245 Main St. #226 - $215,000
      1345 High St. #325 - $275,000
      1345 High St. #328 - $325,000

Many amenities are included in each of these
highly desirable units, making them tremendous
buys. Showings may be arranged for either day or
night by calling us at our office 555-5555.

If you are thinking of selling your present property,
we can offer a marketing program tailored
especially for you. Please feel free to calls us
without obligation.

Sincerely,

CONDOMINIUMS

Date

Name
Address
City, State, Zip

Dear _____,

If in the past year you paid attention to condominiums that were listed and sold in your area, I'm sure you frequently saw ABC Realty signs.

With sales of new and pre-owned condominiums increasing each year, you can be assured that DO IT NOW REALTY has established the background and expertise to facilitate the sale of the fastest growing housing market of the 90's.

With personal sales in excess of $ _____ last year, nearly   25% of my sales involved condominiums. Having been so well received by your community, I am anxious to introduce myself to those who need professional assistance in 1991.

If you would like to know the current market value of your condominium, or if you have any real estate related questions, I would welcome your call and the opportunity to be of service to you.

I look forward to hearing from you.

Sincerely,

Date

Name
Address
City, State, Zip

Dear _____,

There is a new subdivision at _____
which will have wooded lots and (_____) acres of
water. I remembered your interest in boating and
fishing and your desire for a home located on a
waterfront lot. These homesites seem to be just
right for you.

I have information regarding the lots and prices,
so I'll get in touch with you within a few days to set
up a convenient time to look over the plat map.

If you have any friends who would be interested in
this exciting project, I would be happy to pass the
information along to them.

Sincerely,

INTRODUCTION OF NEWSLETTER

Date

Name
Address
City, State, Zip

Dear _____,

Keeping in contact with my friends and past clients have always been important to me, and in this regard I have decided to establish a monthly newsletter beginning in January. This newsletter will be general in nature. It will include information ranging from household hints to recipes, and advice relating to the buying and selling of real estate.

This is simply my way of saying "thank you" on a regular basis for helping me with my business. I will continue to offer the professional service you expect when you or any of your friends need assistance.

Whether you have a specific real estate question or just want to say "hello", I always appreciate your call.

Sincerely,

Date

Name
Address
City, State, Zip

Dear _____,

I'm writing to you concerning real estate. I'm quite sure you've heard a lot from friends or other Realtors in the past few months as to what this industry is all about.

I would like the opportunity to serve you as your Realtor - not just when it's time to buy or sell, but on a continuing basis.

For this reason, I'll be sending you a newsletter periodically that will help keep you abreast of current market conditions, and will include helpful tips about home maintnenance, do-it-yourself projects and items of general interest.

I'd also like to stop by sometime in the near future to meet you. In the meantime, if you have any questions relating to your home or to real estate in general, don't hesitate to give me a call.

Thank You,

Date

Name
Address
City, State, Zip

Dear _____,

I'm writing to you concerning real estate. I'm quite sure you've heard a lot from friends or other Realtors in the past few months as to what this industry is all about.

I would like the opportunity to serve you as your Realtor - not just when it's time to buy or sell, but on a continuing basis.

For this reason, I'll be sending you a newsletter periodically that will help keep you abreast of current market conditions, and will include helpful tips about home maintnenance, do-it-yourself projects and items of general interest.

I'd also like to stop by sometime in the near future to meet you. In the meantime, if you have any questions relating to your home or to real estate in general, don't hesitate to give me a call.

Thank You,

INTRODUCTION OF NEWSLETTER

Date

Name
Address
City, State, Zip

Dear _____,

Your home is probably the largest single investment you'll ever make and considering inflation, one of the wisest. It should interest you to know about the value of your house, its specific market value and the local and national trends that influence its marketability.

Each month, I'll be sending a brief newsletter with pertinent real estate information that could prove to be beneficial when you're ready to buy or sell a home. The material will be capsuled from a variety of local, regional and national sources. I think it will give you an informed perspective of what's happening in real estate today that may sooner or later be pertinent to you.

Sincerely,

PROSPECTING GENERAL

Date

Name
Address
City, State, Zip

Dear _____,

Homebuying and selling are the largest financial decisions that most people make Trust your decision to experienced and seasoned professionals.

Here is a list of just some of the many satisfied customers that I've served:

1. _____, Title_____
2. _____, Title_____
3. _____, Title_____
4. _____, Title _____
5. _____, Title _____

I'll be happy to provide a list of references, just let me know.

Need any of the following on your property:
  a. Your Grant Deed?
  b. Your Plat Map?
  c. Your Loan Documents?
  d. Assessors Record of Sales in Your Area?
  e. A Computer Profile of Your Home's Value?

Call me. No obligation of course. I'll provide you with the documents you may have lost.

It takes no more to hire the best! I'm looking forward to a record 1991.

Sincerely,

Date

Name
Address
City, State, Zip

Dear _____,

A home is probably the largest single investment an individual will make in a lifetime. The decision to buy is a critical one, and deciding how to market your home is just as important.

As an associate with DO IT NOW REALTY, I would like to offer my services in selling your property. We represent many buyers and sellers, and as your exclusive agent, we give your home the attention and exposure it deserves.

As you know, financing requires a thorough understanding of how to obtain mortgage money for prospective buyers. We can offer expertise in this area, and are familiar with the entire range of financing options, current interest rates and conventional money sources.

I would appreciate the opportunity to meet with you to further outline the services I can provide. They include a complimentary market analysis of your home to determine its present market value.

I'll be calling to see if an appointment can be set at your convenience. In the meantime, if I can answer any questions you have about selling your home, please don't hesitate to call me.

Sincerely,

Date

Name
Address
City, State, Zip

Dear _____,

I am contacting several homeowners in your area for information and assistance.

I have buyers that desire a home in your neighborhood. If you or anyone you know is looking to sell their home, I would certainly appreciate if you could let me know. I can help get the job done.

If you would have any questions about real estate, or whether it be to buy, sell, lease or trade-in, please give me a call. I'd be glad to help. Of course, there is no obligation.

Sincerely,

Date

Name
Address
City, State, Zip

Dear _____,

Although we offer our real estate services in all areas, we will be mainly concentrating on a couple of areas where we have been most successful. The Canton area, North Canton area, East Canton area, and South Canton area.

Some of our recent sales in these areas are:

124 Main St.
234 High St.
345 Water St.
456 Park St.
567 Chestnut St.
789 South St.
898 North St.
365 East St.
345 S. Main St.
456 S. Main St.
487 Oak St.

DO IT NOW REALTY is continually working in these areas and we would appreciate the opportunity to talk with you before you consider anyone else should you be looking to buy or sell a home.

Sincerely,

Date

Name
Address
City, State, Zip

Dear _____,

As you may have noticed, there are many DO IT NOW REALTY "For Sale" signs in lawns of homes for sale in your area. We have the reputation of many years of experience in the sale of residential and commercial properties. We also have many satisfied customers that have benefited from our services. We consider every property and every buyer and seller important to us.

When we list a property we offer immediate and long term advantages to our customers. We determine the market value of the property. Approximately 35 licensed Realtors from our company are advised that your home is for sale. We advertise your property for potential buyers, we enter your home in the Multiple Listing Service, which lets all the Realtors in the area know that your home is for sale. We arrange and handle all the appointments to show your property and eliminate curiosity seekers that may be encountered.

Are you in the market at this time to sell your home? If you're not, possibly you could help me. I've enclosed several business cards that can be given to friends or relatives who may be in the market to buy or sell a home, or may be just considering it. There's no obligation. I'd appreciate a call.

Sincerely,

Date

Name
Address
City, State, Zip

Dear _____,

Are you looking to make a move? Are the children getting older?   Looking for a change in neighborhoods? Need convenience? Is your home too small?

Whatever your reason may be, if you're considering making a move, I can help.

I am a Realtor Associate with DO IT NOW REALTY and I would like to help you realize your goals. DO IT NOW REALTY has many years of experience in your area. We can offer you a trade plan that can suit your needs.

May I call on you to explain how a trade-in can work for you. There is no obligation, of course. Call me today and we can set up an appointment at your convenience.

Sincerely,

PROSPECTING GENERAL

Date

Name
Address
City, State, Zip

Dear _____,

Thinking of selling your home? How do you look at the improvements you've made to be able to increase the price you can get for the property?

Basically, look at the initial value of your home. Anything you've done to improve the size, function and attractiveness will increase the value. Also, look at the value of your neighborhood.

When you make room additions with the proper building permits, they have a tendency to get back all your money. If you've made the additions without the proper building permits and the room looks like it was added on, it usually won't increase the value enough to be able to cover your improvements.

These improvements usually will get you a return on your investment, quality kitchen upgrades, new or extra bathrooms, new roofs, wall paper and new windows. These exterior renovations can also add value; exterior paint, siding, shrubs or colorful plants, or concrete or blacktop drive if clean of oil.

These improvements you can hope to break even on; new carpeting, fireplaces, swimming pools, and custom draperies.

So, if you're considering selling your home, call me and I'd like to sit down with you and possibly preview your home to get an idea of what you'll be able to expect.

Sincerely,

Date

Name
Address
City, State, Zip

Dear _____,

Despite today's high interest rates, the demand for housing in your area is very good and today's home buyers realize that their best hedge against inflation is home ownership.

We at _____ have discovered some ideas that are designed to:

1. Market your property and provide you with a qualified buyer.

2. Arrange the financing and handle all the paperwork.

3. Net you the most money possible.

If you are giving any thought to the sale of your property in the near future, we hope we can be of service to you.

Sincerely,

Date

Name
Address
City, State, Zip

Dear _____,

No doubt you have noticed the many homes sold recently in your neighborhood by DO IT NOW REALTY.

Perhaps selling or buying is the furthest thought from your mind at this time, however, children grow . . . homes get too small . . . and families are transferred. So, there may come the time when you, too, want to talk to DO IT NOW REALTY as so many of your neighbors have done.

I have enclosed my business card for your future reference, and I look forward to being of service to you.

Sincerely,

Date

Name
Address
City, State, Zip

Dear _____,

Last spring I sent you a letter introducing myself as your neighbor and as a Real Estate Sales Associate. At this time, I'd like to remind you that I am especially interested in our neighborhood and in the buying and selling of homes in our area.

If you are considering a move within the next few months, or if you know of someone who might be interested in moving into the neighborhood, I'd like to talk with you. I feel we have a lovely and desirable area, and I would like the opportunity to be involved in transactions concerning our neighborhood.

Please call me at any time, either at my home or my office.

Sincerely,

Date

Name
Address
City, State, Zip

Dear _____,

The following is a market update for homes sold
in your area from _____, 19__ to _____,
19__:

During this period, two bedroom homes have sold
for an average of $ _____. Three bedroom
homes have averaged in the upper $ _____'s.
Four bedroom homes from the mid - to high
$ _____'s.

If you have any questions about the present value
of your home, we offer a Market Analysis at no
cost or obligation. This type of evaluation might
be of interest for insurance purposes or just personal
information.

If you have any type of real estate related question,
please give me a call.

Cordially,

Date

Name
Address
City, State, Zip

Dear _____,

I have been working in your neighborhood for a
couple of weeks. I thought I might interest you in
some things what will directly effect the value of
your property. Your property's value will coincide
with the general market conditions and overall
economy of the area.

However, the specific value of your home will
only matter to you when you want to either sell it
or borrow against it. Any property will be worth
what the buyer is willing to pay for it., nothing
more nothing less. If someone tells you "It's not
worth that much", if the buyers are paying for it
and the lenders are supporting it, then it is worth
that much. When they aren't, it isn't.

Another factor which effects the value of a property
is the reason for selling. When there is a strong
reason, the price will be more realistic and the sale
will be more likely. If the reason is weak, the price
will be higher and the less likely the sale.

If you've been considering a move, please call me
and we can go over what pertains to your own
circumstances.

Thank you,

FARMING LETTER

Date

Name
Address
City, State, Zip

Dear _____,

I want to introduce myself and let you know that
you will be seeing me in your neighborhood.

I am familiar with your neighborhood and with the
homes and it's values. This is a very desirable area
and that is why I've chosen it to help bring good
people into, as well as help anyone leaving this
area to find an area just as suitable as this one.

As I'm working here, I will learn all about the
neighborhood and why people will want to live
there. I will be on top of any changes such as,
construction, general changes in the economy,
and even what's going on in the school district. My
job is to be aware of anything that effects the value
of your home and your neighborhood.

If there is anything I can do for you or any
questions that I might answer, please feel free to
call me. In turn, if there is anything you think that
I should be aware of that might help me as I try to
find suitable neighbors for your area.

Sincerely,

Date

Name
Address
City, State, Zip

Dear _____,

This is a letter of introduction.

My name is _____. I am a residential sales specialist with (Your Company Name)

I will be working to become an expert on the _____ neighborhood, and I hope that you will come to feel that you have a "friend in the business" that you can call on for real estate help.

I'll be in the neighborhood in the near future, and look forward to an opportunity to meet you.

Have a great day.

Sincerely,

NEIGHBOR TO A NEW LISTING

Date

Name
Address
City, State, Zip

Dear _____,

As you probably know, your neighbors at 1234 Main St. have their home listed for sale with DO IT NOW REALTY.

I've shown their home to two different families, and although that particular home did not suit their needs, both families want to live in your area. I am trying to find a home for them somewhere nearby.

If you are contemplating a move anytime in the near future, I would appreciate the opportunity to talk with you. I'll be telephoning you in the next few days to introduce myself and to discuss the outstanding services that DO IT NOW REALTY offers.

Sincerely,

Date

Name
Address
City, State, Zip

Dear _____,

Your neighbors, Mrs. & Mrs. John Smith, have enlisted my help to sell their home at 1234 Main St.

I am trying to find someone who will be a congenial neighbor for you. It has occurred to me that since you will be interested in the outcome of this sale, you might like to suggest a friend or a relative who may be in the market for such a home.

If you know of anyone who would like to view this type home, please don't hesitate to contact me at my residence or office at any time. I am most grateful for any assistance that you can give me.

Sincerely,

Date

Name
Address
City, State, Zip

Dear _____,

As you may have already noticed, I am representing Mr. & Mrs. Smith in the sale of their home at 1234 Main St.

My custom in marketing a home as thoroughly as possible is to reach as many prospective buyers as I can.

If you happen to know of anyone who might be interested in the Smith's home, or if you wish to inquire about it yourselves, just give me a call. I'll be glad to help.

Sincerely,

Date

Name
Address
City, State, Zip

Dear _____,

I thought perhaps you would be interested to know that I have just listed the John Smith property on Main St. in North Canton.

This very large and interesting house has seven bedrooms and nine baths, and an elevator to the second floor. A two bedroom suite on the main level overlooks a walled rose garden.

I recently sold the former Jones home on High St. and the Miller home on Cherry St., and participated in the sale of the Taylor property on Chestnut St. I have been active in the North Canton market for many years and know how in demand properties such as these are.

If you would like to inspect this home, or if you would like an invitation to a private Open House planned for the near future, or if I may be of assistance with any real estate needs you may have, please call me at my office on Main St., 555-5555 or after hours at 555-5555.

Sincerely,

Date

Name
Address
City, State, Zip

Dear _____,

This letter is to inform you that I have placed Mr.
Jones's home, located at 134 Main St., on the
market for sale. This is a very nice home, and we
have a very attractive price on it. If you know of
anyone who would be interested in purchasing
this very lovely home, I would appreciate it very
much if you would have them call me.

Also, if you are interested in selling your home, or
know of someone who is interested in selling their
home, I would be happy to make a Free Market
Value Report to determine what the home would
bring on the market.

Sincerely,

Date

Name
Address
City, State, Zip

Dear _____,

Here is your chance to choose a new neighbor for your lovely neighborhood.

I have just listed a Main St. bargain, and it is gorgeous!

This 3 bedroom 2 bath home features, 2400 sq. ft. of living area, with a 1 1/2 car garage. Privacy abounds in the rear yard. Slight updating needed to make this bargain into a beauty. Estate sale price reflects the anxious heirs! Call for a brochure or an appointment.

Perhaps you know of someone who would like to enjoy the lifestyle to which you've become accustomed. A friend, a family member or perhaps yourself (as an investment) or maybe you know of someone interested in selling their home. I would appreciate hearing from you.

Sincerely,

P.S. Need at NOTARY? As part of my service to the community I offer FREE notary service.

Date

Name
Address
City, State, Zip

Dear _____,

By now you've probably noticed the DO IT NOW REALTY "For Sale" sign in your neighbors lawn on _____.

Possibly, you've even wondered about whether you might be interested in making a move. You've obviously chosen this neighborhood for a reason and that's why you're still here. However, maybe your needs as a family have changed and this home might be able to suit your new needs.

I'd be happy to take you through this property and let you know what your home would be worth. Give me a call and we can set up an appointment to view Mr. & Mrs. Jones' home.

Sincerely,

Date

Name
Address
City, State, Zip

Dear _____,

We have just listed your neighbor's property on
_____.   There has been
interest on this property and your neighborhood.

We are showing this property to prospective buyers
who, in actuality, will be your new neighbors.
Here's where you can help. If anyone you know is
interested in living in your neighborhood or would
know of anyone who might be interested in this
home, please feel free to call me. After all, it's
your neighborhood.

Sincerely,

Date

Name
Address
City, State, Zip

Dear _____,

We have been chosen by Mr. & Mrs. Smith to assist them in marketing their home on 1234 Main St. The location, condition and scale of this exceptional home may be the ideal choice for one of your friends who may be seeking the special enjoyment of living in your neighborhood.

We invite you and your friends to call us for an appointment to preview this fine home and learn more about it's special features.

Sincerely,

Date

Name
Address
City, State, Zip

Dear _____,

We are pleased to inform you that Jane Smith has just sold the   DO IT NOW REALTY listing located at 1234 Main St. Mr. & Mrs. Jones from Canton, Ohio are the new owners.

Jane Smith has just completed her ninth and most successful year in real estate. During 1989, she closed more than 10 Million Dollars in residential property. Several of these home were located in your area. Through April of 1990, Jane closed and/or booked over 4 Million Dollars in residential sales.

We hope you are aware that in addition to our other offices, DO IT NOW REALTY has two locations in your area. If you are interested in a current market analysis on your property, please do not hesitate to call Jane at the office 555-5555 or home 555-5555.

Sincerely,

NEIGHBOR TO SOLD

Date

Name
Address
City, State, Zip

Dear _____,

As you probably know, the Jones' home at 1234 Main St. was recently sold. We would like to take this opportunity to introduce your new neighbors, John & Jane Smith. The Smiths will be moving here from the Canton, Ohio area. Please introduce yourself and make the Smiths feel welcome in their new neighborhood.

DO IT NOW REALTY is happy to have had the opportunity to represent the Smith's purchase of their new home. We feel fortunate to have been able to locate them in a desirable neighborhood such as yours.

We have many other clients who are just as interested in buying a home in your area but who, for various reasons, are not satisfied with the few homes that are now available. If you know of anyone thinking of selling their home or who is being transferred, please let me know.

I will be contacting you soon by telephone, and any help you can give me would be much appreciated.

Sincerely,

Date

Name
Address
City, State, Zip

Dear _____,

Please join us in welcoming your new neighbors,
_____. Many families had
the opportunity to meet _____and their
daughter/son(s) _____at the recent
neighborhood picnic. The _____have
purchased the home of _____ at
_____.

(Former residents name) are enjoying their new
home at _____ and wish to be
remembered to their many friends here.

Cordially,

51

Date

Name
Address
City, State, Zip

Dear _____,

We did it!

We were successful in finding a buyer for the property at _____. During the course of marketing this listing, we found several other interested purchasers who might be interested in a similar property or location.

If you've ever thought of selling or exchanging, now may be the right time. Give me a call for a confidential no-obligation analysis of your real estate investment. We'll help you calculate your present pre-tax and after-tax yields and give you some valuable information on determining the best time to sell and reinvest.

Sincerely,

Date

Name
Address
City, State, Zip

Dear _____,

I am pleased to announce that my listing at 1234 Main St. was sold and closed this past week to a lovely couple who have many friends already living in your area.

Through advertising, open houses and accompanying personal showings of this property, I have acquired many additional customers for your area.

If you have been considering the sale of your home or lot, I would be happy to meet with you at your convenience to discuss market values, etc.

I am dedicated to providing you exceptional service from the initial listing of your property through a smooth and successful closing.

Please feel free to call anytime at my office or at my home.

I sincerely look forward to hearing from you now or in the future.

Sincerely,

Date

Name
Address
City, State, Zip

Dear _____,

I've just sold the home at 1234 Main St. in your neighborhood.

Your new neighbors are Mr. & Mrs. Bill Jones. They will be moving within the month. They are excited to be moving into this area. Won't you please welcome them?

In working with Mr. & Mrs. Smith to sell this home, I have come across other clients that are also interested in this area. So, if you or anyone you know of is interested in selling their house, please give me a call.

If I can be of any service to you whether it be buying or selling a home, let me know.

Sincerely,

Date

Name
Address
City, State, Zip

Dear _____,

Until I have the opportunity of meeting you, please allow this letter to serve as an introduction.

I am a sales associate with DO IT NOW REALTY specializing in listing and selling residential real estate - lots, land and homes.

In today's real estate market, there is a constant demand for good building sites for single family dwellings as well as land suited to sub-dividing for residential developments.

It is my hope that we can arrange an appointment at your convenience to discuss your thoughts for the development of your property. I'm confident our services can help you realize the greatest potential and highest return on your investment.

I look forward to the opportunity of visiting with you.

Sincerely,

Date

Name
Address
City, State, Zip

Dear _____,

It has been my pleasure to handle your real estate needs over the past years. Many people have referred their friends and business associates to me, for which I am grateful. These references have played a big part in my success.

This is just a friendly reminder that we are once again entering a prime real estate market, and I look forward to serving those preferred referrals once again.

If you do know of someone who is planning to buy, sell or build, I would appreciate if you would you call. Thank you for your time and continuing help.

Sincerely,

Date

Name
Address
City, State, Zip

Dear _____,

I sincerely hope that the sale of your previous home and the purchase of the new one was a satisfactory transaction for you. I appreciate the opportunity of being able to assist you.

As buying a home is one of the most important decisions you'll make, I hope that you will be pleased with the decision you made and that you will spend many years of happiness in your new residence. I'm thankful for the confidence that you showed in me.

I pride myself on my continuing service even after the sale. Never hesitate to call me if you have any questions or need advice on this property or in any other matter of real estate.

I would appreciate that if you know of anyone that is looking to buy or sell a home, that you recommend me to them. I would like to be able to offer them the same service that I was able to give you and your family.

Good luck in your new home,

PROSPECTING FOR REFERRAL

Date

Name
Address
City, State, Zip

Dear _____,

We are enjoying an active real estate market in our area this season, and why not? Most people find owning property here pretty exciting. I certainly do!

If you know friends who will soon be in the market as buyers or sellers in this area, won't you please recommend that they give me a call; or if you will get in touch with me, I'll call them.

I truly appreciate the recommendation of my old and new friends. They have been very good to me (to the tune of over six million in sales per year) and I count on them to continue to remember me favorably. In return, they, and you, can count on me to continue to give V.I.P. service to those friends referred to me.

Please call the next time you are in the area, if only to say hello.

Sincerely,

Date

Name
Address
City, State, Zip

Dear _____,

Your name was given to me by a mutual acquaintance so that I could be of help with your move to the area. To that end, I am enclosing our Newcomer's Guide.

The Guide provides an overview of the Canton, Ohio area, covering everything from education to entertainment. Also included are practical tips to make your move a little easier and an introduction to what our area has to offer.

I have also enclosed a sample of homes for sale in the area that I feel may be of some interest to you in the price range you're looking for and the area you wish to relocate to.

I will call you in a few days to answer any questions you might have and to find out how I can be of further help. In the meantime, I hope our Newcomer's Guide will be of interest to you and will help you familiarize yourself with the Canton area, which will be your new home.

Sincerely,

Date

Name
Address
City, State, Zip

Dear _____,

Good Day! No matter whether it's morning, afternoon or evening, at your convenience, I can assist you in relocation. DO IT NOW REALTY has been in business in this area for 25 years, and we built our business on satisfying customers such as yourself.

In our Multiple Listing Service we have over 2,000 homes available in this area from which to choose. Our company along ha 215 available listings that we can show you.

I've enclosed my card and a brochure on a couple of listings that have just been listed on the market. I would very much like to be of service to you in this area. Also enclosed is a copy of a Guide which promotes what the Stark County area has to offer including entertainment, dining, schooling, banking, local business and much more!

Please give me a call!

Sincerely,

Date

Name
Address
City, State, Zip

Dear _____,

The end of the year will be here soon, and I want
you to know what a pleasure it is serving the needs
of your transferred employees. The confidence
you have placed in my service has made it possible
for my business to grow steadily and rapidly. In
turn, perhaps a contented employee has contributed
to the growth and success of your business.

Thanks again for your confidence in me. I hope
you and yours have a happy holiday season and a
prosperous new year.

Thank you,

Date

Name
Address
City, State, Zip

Dear _____,

As a follow-up to our recent telephone conversation, I have enclosed literature describing how your company could benefit from enlisting the services of a DO IT NOW REALTY representative.

I would like the opportunity to meet with you further to discuss becoming your company's real estate advisor. I'll be in contact with you in the near future to schedule an appointment at your convenience.

I'm looking forward to meeting with you and to establish a close working relationship with you and your corporation.

Thank you,

Date

Name
Address
City, State, Zip

Dear _____,

I appreciate you taking the time to speak with me on Monday. I'm sure your employees appreciate that you are always thinking of new ways to serve them.

Real estate consulting is a very valuable service to offer your employees. As that consultant, I can inform them on the latest real estate trends and can contribute information to your company newsletter when needed. The seminars will be conducted at the convenience of the employees and on site. All of these services, which include consultations, articles, and seminars will be provided to employees of your company at no charge.

I feel that by having one person who is familiar with the real estate market is a great benefit.

I have completed the preparation of your program and will give you a call to set an appointment so we can review it. You will be one of the first to offer this unique service to ALL of your people.

I am looking forward to working with your company and its employees.

Sincerely,

Date

Name
Address
City, State, Zip

Dear _____,

Real Estate in the Stark County area is better than ever! There were ____ sales last year, and our company alone sold ____ homes. We are pleased to be Number One in the area. The average selling price in Stark County is _____.

We have developed a marketing program to assist employees in their real estate needs. For any employees moving out of the area we offer a National Relocation Service and for any employees moving into the area we offer a Guide To Stark County.

If we can be of any service to your company or your employees at any time, please feel free to give us a call. We'd be happy to meet with you and show you what we can offer.

Sincerely,

Date

Name
Address
City, State, Zip

Dear _____,

We've got good news about your neighborhood! Our company has just listed the property at 1234 Main St. for sale and thought you might be interested in previewing it before we actually place it on the market.

If you have ever thought about acquiring an additional real estate property for income, tax shelter, business or expansion purposes, please give me a call. I'd be happy to arrange a confidential inspection of the property and furnish you with additional information.

At the same time, if you've thought of selling, refinancing or exchanging your present building, I'd be pleased to perform a complimentary investment analysis outlining your present pre-tax and after-tax rate of returns for now and in the future.

Very truly yours,

Date

Name
Address
City, State, Zip

Dear _____,

I had the privilege of recently being involved with a meeting on the Park Avenue Development. This will be a new office park (or shopping center) located at Park Avenue and High Avenue.

If you know of any company that would be interested in buying or leasing in this area, this is a fine location. I would appreciate if you could give them my name or call me.

Carmel, Inc. is the agent for this project, and they are cooperating with all Realtors.

If you know of someone who might be interested, please have them give me a call.

Sincerely,

Date

Name
Address
City, State, Zip

Dear _____,

I have been made aware that you are interested in purchasing some land for your company.

The land that I have listed is _____ acres and is very competitively priced at _____ a quare foot. If you're looking to build, this wou... be a very good location for your company. The property is located on High Ave. and is very accessible from all parts of the city, including the expressway. There is also street access as well.

I will give you a call in a couple days and we can discuss this further.

Sincerely,

Date

Name
Address
City, State, Zip

Dear _____,

It has come to my attention that you own the property located at 124 High Ave. A mutual associate, John Smith, mentioned that you might be interested in selling this property. I work with many investors and would definitely like to talk to you about the possibility. I am confident that I could sell this very easily.

I would appreciate a call from you when it's convenient. I've enclosed my business card. I'd like to get the necessary facts so that I would work up a Broker's Reconstruction Form for you. This form takes all costs and income into consideration so that we can arrive at a competitive market price for this property.

Please give me a call when you can.

Sincerely,

Date

Name
Address
City, State, Zip

Dear _____,

As homeowners, you are undoubtedly aware of the importance of your investment. In fact, real estate continues to be just about the best hedge against inflation that is available today.

If you've lived in your home for over a year, chances are good that you may not be aware of its current market value. If this is the case, I'd like to offer you a free Market Analysis.

A Market Analysis is an estimate of the current fair market value of your home. This estimate will be based on a comprehensive study done of similar homes in this area, including those homes currently on the market and those that have sold in the past few months.

Knowing the current market value of your home is helpful even if you're not planning to sell in the near future. It's an important step in re-evaluating your insurance coverage to protect the ever-increasing value of your investment.

As a resident of the area, I am offering this service to you at no cost or obligation, but simply as a means of introducing myself. Please call me and we'll arrange a time that's convenient for you.

Sincerely,

Name
Address
City, State, Zip

Dear _____,

There's no such thing as a free lunch!

But there is a free investment analysis available for your real estate property. This analysis should help you calculate your present pre-tax and after-tax returns and help you determine the optimal time to sell or exchange.

Our specialty is investment real estate. Let us show you how we can serve you.

Sincerely,

Date

Name
Address
City, State, Zip

Dear _____,

I noticed your garage sale this week. Garage sales
in our area usually draw excellent responses, and
I'm sure your sales efforts were well rewarded.

I've found that quite often the sale of household
items precedes the sale of real estate. If you are
considering the sale of your home, may I take this
opportunity to offer the professional services of
DO IT NOW REALTY?

If you would like to know the current market value
of your home, our company makes complimentary
market evaluations of residential properties. If
this service would be helpful to your family at this
time, please feel free to contact me either at home
or at my office.

Thank you,

Date

Name
Address
City, State, Zip

Dear _____,

Today's paper indicated the recent loss of your beloved. I'm very sorry and I wish you comfort and peace during these trying times.

I'm deliberately avoiding a personal contact to you at this time, Mrs. Jones. I hardly think that would be appropriate. Instead, I'm enclosing my business card should you like to discuss business matters at any time, now or in the future. . . I am at your service.

Again, I offer my condolences.

Sincerely,

Date

Name
Address
City, State, Zip

Dear _____,

I noticed your "For Sale By Owner" sign today and
I am admittedly curious about what activity it has
generated for you.

Your home is a property I would like to have in my
"inventory" to market. However, I pride myself on
the fact that I personally maintain only five listings
for sale at a time. I feel that is the maximum
number any agent can handle if he is to be fair to,
and do an effective job for, the home sellers they
represent.

Since I have five listings now, it is really premature
for me to discuss representing you, but when one
of my current listings sells, I will contact you.

Good Luck!

PROSPECTING FSBO

Date

Name
Address
City, State, Zip

Dear _____,

I heard recently that you were hoping to sell your home. Obviously you have made the decision not to use a Realtor at this time, and I understand and respect that decision.

During the time you are working to sell your house, I hope you will let me "touch bases" with you from time to time. I have enclosed some material for your review:

• Two blank sales contracts;

• Buyer's statements which may help you show the buyer what his costs will be at closing;

•Information on some available financing programs.

I will be happy to visit with you and perhaps suggest some methods to effect a sale which will be specifically tailored to your situation.

I have assisted other sellers in this manner, and have retained their confidence because I do not pressure them to "list" their property. In many cases, sellers grow weary of the amount of time and expense involved and have asked me. to represent them. I ask only that if you change your mind and want a professional approach to selling, that you consider me and my company. If, in the meantime, I can help you in any way, please, don't hesitate to call.

Sincerely Yours,

Date

Name
Address
City, State, Zip

Dear _____,

I saw your "For Sale" sign today and wonder what progress you have made so far toward getting your home sold.

From the number of (<u>Your company name</u>) "For Sale" and "Sold" signs you have seen in your neighborhood, you are probably aware that our company has the greatest number of homes in your area to offer our clients. Because we have more homes to offer our clients, we also attract the largest number of homebuying prospects. Quite possibly, among our clients is the very family who needs a home just like yours.

Would you like me to show your home to my clients? Give it some thought, and I'll be in touch with you soon.

Sincerely,

PROSPECTING FSBO

Date

Name
Address
City, State, Zip

Dear _____,

I was in your neighborhood today and noticed your "For Sale" sign. Your home is very attractive, and I hope you are getting good activity from interested prospects. The fee you save by selling your property yourself would look great in your bank account! But do you really save? Consider the following:

• There are legal fees when it is time to close. We can save you money on many of those costs.

• You will be faced with expensive newspaper advertising. We can assume this expense for you.

• Negotiating with tough-minded buyers can be a frustrating experience, and often a costly one. We are specialists in negotiating real estate sales.

• Valuable time can be wasted in dealing with prospective buyers who cannot secure financing. We would show your home only to prospects we have qualified financially.

Our company specializes in the sale of property for homeowners. We know the market, and we know what it takes to sell a house. I hope you will give me an opportunity to explain our proven marketing program soon. There is no obligation, of course.

Sincerely,

Date

Name
Address
City, State, Zip

Dear _____,

It has recently come to my attention that you are trying to market your home.

I have enclosed a brochure along with my business card.

If you have any questions concerning real estate, please don't hesitate to call me.

Sincerely,

Date

Name
Address
City, State, Zip

Dear _____,

It was nice meeting you - even if it was on the phone.

Believe me, I'm being completely honest in wishing you success in selling your home yourself.

A great many people are successful in selling without the assistance of professionals. You can be too - if you follow several basic principles and learn what to do and what not to do.

Those who fail in their attempts to sell themselves fail because they make mistakes - mistakes which could be avoided.

We have a service which is unique in this area. We provide owners who are selling their homes themselves with a "Homeowner's Sales Kit". It contains a list of the things you should do and should not do if you are to meet with success. It also includes many of the special forms you will require. It can be quite valuable to you.

We believe this "special service" is the best advertising we can do for our company, so there is no charge and no obligation.

Hopefully, you will be appreciative and do business with us someday.

Why not let us help you? Call me at 555-5555, and I'll deliver the kit in person - and I promise not to try to sell you on listing with us.

Sincerely,

Date

Name
Address
City, State, Zip

Dear _____,

I'm sincerely grateful to you for the opportunity you gave me to present our unique service.

If you follow the advice and the rules which I've given you, your chances of being successful will be greatly improved.

If you encounter questions and problems which puzzle you, please don't hesitate to call me. I was completely sincere when I said "I want to help you in every way I possibly can."

If your personal situation changes and you decide to employ a real estate professional to assist you, I do hope you will give me consideration. At least, I would like an opportunity to show you how we would go about marketing your home, the things we would do for you which you can't very well do for yourself, and why we have earned the reputation of being one of the most successful, reputable and reliable real estate agencies in this part of the country.

We want to be of help to you now - and in the future.

Sincerely,

Date

Name
Address
City, State, Zip

Dear _____,

Noticing your ad in the newspaper, I am sending you this letter to introduce myself and my company.

We, at DO IT NOW REALTY, have ways to protect your family, to make the sale of your property faster and easier, and to help net you the most money.

I will be in contact with you soon to discuss these ideas which I am sure you will find helpful.

Sincerely,

Date

Name
Address
City, State, Zip

Dear _____,

When I drove past your house today I noticed your "For Sale By Owner" sign. I understand you want the opportunity to sell your home yourself, but I honestly believe I can save you considerable time and expense if you will let me go to work for you.

My company and I have the prospects, the knowledge of available financing and current market values, and an outstanding advertising program, all of which will enable you to get "top dollar" from the sale of your home.

Give it some thought. I'll be in touch with you in a day or two for an appointment to preview your home.

Sincerely,

PROSPECTING FSBO

Date

Name
Address
City, State, Zip

Dear _____,

If you have sold your property by now, we congratulate you! If not, learn how we can serve you.

Selling your own property is at best a difficult task. In order to conclude a satisfactory sale in today's competitive real estate market, professional help is needed to deal with many problems of evaluations, advertising, qualifying prospects, mortgages, conveyances of title, financing sources, title insurance continuation, taxes and closing details. The knowledge and experience of a Realtor to motivate a prospect into positive action can relieve you of such burden.

Our 26 offices have contacts with major industries and have ready access to out-of-town as well as local purchasers. In addition, you will benefit from our extensive advertising program and our efforts to protect your privacy. Only qualified prospects will inspect your home.

When we list your home for sale, an aggressive sales campaign is immediately launched, but it costs you nothing unless we conclude a satisfactory sale.

In 10 years at DO IT NOW REALTY, I have served many clients and have closed over _____ transactions. I would appreciate an opportunity to discuss in person the benefits we can offer. Please phone me at your convenience for an appointment to discuss the most profitable way to market your home.

Sincerely,

Date

Name
Address
City, State, Zip

Dear _____,

I've noticed that you've had your own "for sale" sign on your home for quite some time. May I have just a moment of your time to explain why it might be the time to trade your sign for one of ours?

Consider the inconvenience and the time you spend showing your home to those who make a hobby of looking - with no intention of buying.

Negotiations with a tough-minded buyer can be both frustrating and a costly experience for you. At best, you can only spend part of your time trying to sell your home while I spend all of my time working with buyers and sellers.

People are known for the company they keep. We are known by the thousands of satisfied families who have sold or purchased a home through our company.

I would welcome the opportunity to personally explain our marketing program and how we can change that "for sale" sign in your front yard to a DO IT NOW REALTY "SOLD" sign.

Sincerely,

Date

Name
Address
City, State, Zip

Dear _____,

I see by the sign in your lawn that you are trying
to sell your home yourself. Maybe you can
accomplish this and again maybe not. Usually
selling your home yourself results in frustration
and difficulties.

Surveys show that the person who lists their home
with a Realtor usually gets more for their home
and with fewer headaches.

If you advertise your home, you will get some
calls. Will they be from ready, willing and able
buyers? Not usually. Many will not give you their
name; some will be just curious; appointments
don't show up, they just drive by and look around.
Buyers are looking to eliminate their options.
They will want information on the home and the
price and then usually will thank you and hang up.
If you do set up an appointment, do you know who
you are actually letting into your home? Is that
safe?

Do you know how to handle financing questions,
appraisal questions, second mortgages, etc.

When you list with an experienced Realtor with an
established firm such as DO IT NOW REALTY,
the time consuming frustrations you will
experience can be avoided.

We handle the phone calls, we professionally
appraise your property, we do the advertising, we

. . . continued

. . . continued

qualify the buyers, we have ready, willing and able buyers, we show your home when it's convenient for you, we assist with the financing problems and questions, and we handle your headaches.

Since you pay nothing unless we sell your home, what do you have to lose? All of the Realtors in our Multiple Listing Service also have buyers that they are working with, that will be working to sell your home as well.

We at DO IT NOW REALTY have the knowledge and experience to get the job done for you. My goal is to sell your home as quickly as possible, for the best price and with the least amount of hassle possible.

Why not give me a call? We can sit down and discuss what your goals and objectives are.

Sincerely,

Date

Name
Address
City, State, Zip

Dear _____,

I've enclosed a copy of your ad on your home that ran in the newspaper on the same day that we ran the other enclosed ad on one of our listings. The home we advertised SOLD!

Why? There really is no mystery as to why some houses sell and some don't. I am a full time Realtor and work hard to sell my listings as do the other _____ agents in our local Board of Realtors. These other agents will be working with buyers who will be interested in your home if you list with me.

I will call you in a few days to set up an appointment to discuss an opportunity that you don't want to miss.

Sincerely,

Date

Name
Address
City, State, Zip

Dear _____,

The classified ad offering your home for sale caught my eye in today's paper. I am looking for a home for my clients who want to locate in your area, and your house sounds like one in which they might be interested. They are moving here from out-of-state (or town) and have asked me to find a home that meets their needs.

Would it be possible for me to drop by to see your hoe in the next few days? I'll call first to arrange a convenient time and, of course, there is no obligation.

Thank You,

Date

Name
Address
City, State, Zip

Dear _____,

I noticed a couple of weeks ago that you've been trying to sell your home yourself.

Let me share with you some facts that you may want to consider. In your area there are over 350 full time real estate salespeople, all whom are working 7 days a week to sell homes. Many of these homes are in your home's price range. The average selling time for a home in your price range is 120 days. These 350 salespeople have between them a vast number of potential buyers. Don't you think you should consider the length of time it could take you, working part time, to sell your home.

We feel that with our experience, we could be a financial advantage to you.

We know what you should do to show your home to the best advantage. You need to be able to think like a buyer, whom we work with daily, and not like a seller.

We also are able to help you with pricing to be able to get you the best price in the shortest time possible.

I think we can help. If you're interested in sitting down and seeing what we have to offer, give me a call at 555-5555. There's no obligation.

Sincerely,

Date

Name
Address
City, State, Zip

Dear _____,

I see by the sign in your lawn you have gone into
the real estate business as myself. Hopefully, your
experience will be successful, but brief. In the
case that it's not, you may decide to turn the job
over to an expert.

Maybe you don't understand what I do. My job is
helping people get what they want.   I arrange the
best sale to fit the circumstances, CLOSE the sale,
and in a timely manner. Because I am experienced
in this, I can ususally foresee any problems before
they come up and can help avoid these problems
that may prevent you from selling or closing on the
sale of your home.

Here's how I can help:

Because the #1 reason that the sale fails is buyer
financing problems. We can show you how to
qualify your buyer in advance.

The #2 reason for failure is the low appraisal that
scares away the lender. We can help you arrive at
the right price.

Because we know the marketplace, we can
share with you what period of time you can expect
the sale to take.

These are just a couple of reasons why we suggest
that you   consider making an appointment with
us. Won't you give us a call today at 555-5555.

Sincerely,

PROSPECTING FSBO

Date

Name
Address
City, State, Zip

Dear _____,

I've been noticing by the sign in your lawn that you've been trying to sell your home for a while. If you're able to do that, all fine and good. But because of the length of time that has gone by, I'm sure that you're behind the time you were initially looking at when you first put the sign in your lawn.

Because my specialty is helping people do what you are trying to do, I'm good at getting homes sold. I'll either get the job done for you or tell you why I can't.

Here's why I've been so successful in the past with my buyers. They know that even after the sale, when you're long gone, I'm here to help them if there's a problem. It doesn't cost them any more to work with me. I'm a full time professional and they trust me because I know what I'm doing.

I don't get paid until the job is done. There's never a question of what it costs you to do the job to your satisfaction.

I have a list of references from people I've worked with in the past, both buyers and sellers. I also have a step-by-step marketing plan for the properties I represent that differs from any that you can do yourself.

If you're interested in my stopping by or would like a list of references, please feel free to call me. Of course, there's no obligation.

Sincerely,

Date

Name
Address
City, State, Zip

Dear _____,

I saw your ad in last Sunday's paper and am aware
that you are trying to sell your home yourself.
Would you please take a couple minutes to review
below the advantages of working with a Realtor.

1. The average homeowner does not actually
know the true market value. As a Realtor, I have
the knowledge of the market and can assist in this.

2. Surveys show that homes that are sold by the
owner do not net as much as homes that are sold by
Realtors.

3. A Realtor works with loan companies on a daily
basis and are aware of the best possible financing
benefits to the buyer and the seller. There are
many many ways to finance a home, and I can
show you the one that will benefit you and your
situation the best.

4. A Realtor knows how to overrule the objections
of a home buyer. Chances are they will ask
questions of a Realtor they would not ask the
homeowner.

5. Are you familiar with title insurance, code
inspections, discount points, documentary stamps?
There are many more. If you don't, this transaction
could possibly be more complicated than you may
anticipate.

6. Realtors have a Multiple Listing Service

. . . continued

... continued

that lets all of the Realtors who are working with
many many buyers, know that your home is for
sale. You'll not have one, but many Realtors
working for you. Are you waiting for someone to
call on your ad or drive by your home? We have
ready, willing and able buyers already available.

7. We can qualify the buyer. We can handle the
personal matters that are not often talked about
that may influence the sale.

8. Are you advertising your home? What are you
spending? Not only can your home appear in our
Multiple Listing Service, but we have many
means of advertising that will attract buyers. And
we pay for it.

After reviewing these points, if you have any
questions of how I can be of greater service to you
please call me. I'd be glad to sit down with you and
you're under no obligation.

Sincerely,

Date

Name
Address
City, State, Zip

I understand your desire to continue to offer your home for sale yourself.

Since there could be the possibility that you may consider at some point in time to use the services of a Realtor, I would like very much to have an appointment with you to explain our marketing program which has proven so successful, and to put the full resources of our company to work for you. We offer:

• A sales staff or over 300 full-time professionally trained associates.
• Membership in all Multiple Listing Associations in the area, as well as a referral service whereby we are in contact with brokers across the nation.
• Most importantly . . . a record of success in getting properties sold which is unmatched in the area. (Details of this record are part of our listing presentation.)

At your convenience, I welcome the opportunity of meeting with you and look forward to hearing from you soon.

Sincerely,

PROSPECTING FSBO

Date

Name
Address
City, State, Zip

I can see by the sign in your lawn that you are trying to sell your home yourself. I hope you have had some measure of success. However, if you are in need of help, I'd like to express my genuine eagerness to be of assistance.

As you may have discovered by now, selling ones own home involves a certain amount of inconvenience, and occasionally, considerable frustration. This can be avoided through a planned, cooperative sales program, beginning with professional evaluation.

The evaluation and selling of real estate is a field for specialists - people with experience and solid background. Anyone can make a investment, but the figure will be no more significant than the level of experience of the person who makes it.

The listing evaluation which I offer you is backed up by the comprehensive knowledge of our full-time sales professionals. Our Market Value Analysis is yours for the mere asking - without any obligation on your part.

Please call me at 555-5555.

Sincerely,

Date

Name
Address
City, State, Zip

Dear _____,

We are in the same business. The business of selling homes. However, I am also in the business of watching for properties for sale and I noticed the "For Sale" sign in your lawn. Obviously, if you had been interested in the service of a Real Estate Professional, you would have listed your home for sale with one of the local Realtor Offices in our area.

We have found, however, that many people that are trying to sell their own home eventually do decide to list their homes with a Realtor. For this reason, I'd like to share with you what we can offer you:

a. We're serious about what we do. We have many buyers and need more homes to show them.

b. We arrange for the financing on homes.

c. We have an advertising program as part of our marketing strategy.

d. We have many out-of-town buyers as well as local buyers.

e. We have your home professionally appraised.

f. We have a Multiple Listing Service that lets all of the Realtors in the area, who are working with many buyers, know that your home is for sale.

. . . continued

. . . continued

g. We have an entire office of full-time professionals that will be working for you as well.

h. We've been in this business since 1954.

Please let us know if we can be of any help to you in selling your home.

Sincerely,

Date

Name
Address
City, State, Zip

Dear _____,

I noticed from the sign in the lawn that your home has been for sale for a while now.

As you by now have realized, selling your home is complicated, frustrating and very time consuming. If you have reached the point that you may be considering asking the help of a Realtor, please keep me in mind.

You may have noticed the many DO IT NOW REALTY "For Sale" signs in your neighborhood. We have had great success here. We have many buyers that are interested in this area and are looking for more homes to be able to show them.

Should you consider using the services of a Real Estate Professional, I would appreciate it if you keep me in mind. I'd be glad to talk to you. You are under no obligation, of course.

Sincerely,

PROSPECTING

EXPIRED
LISTINGS

Prospecting the Expired Listing
is Understanding the Expired Listing!

6 out of 10 expired listings will re-list with
another Realtor within the first 30 days
from when their listing expired. This is
bad new for those Realtors who lost the
listing and good news for those few
Realtors who have chosen to seek out,
contact, and pick up the expired listing as
a new listing.

You now have in your hands many
successful model letters to improve your
strategy of building a listing inventory.
These letters can be effective in your
approach of prospecting the expired
listing. You may use one of these letters or
a series of letters to achieve your objective.

Date

Name
Address
City, State, Zip

Dear _____,

In speaking with you on Monday, and going over
the listing sheet on your property, I am more
confused than ever as to why your house did not
sell. I am sure you must be even more confused
than I. The key to moving property in this market
is repeated showings to the right buyers. That is
our specialty.

The proposal that I promised you is nearly
complete, and I will have it ready by our meeting.
This includes the four step plan for quickly selling
your property and the honest written appraisal.

I will call on Monday, Feb. 2nd to arrange the most
convenient time for a meeting.

Sincerely,

P.S. Could you be ready to move on April 1st?

PROSPECTING EXPIRED LISTING

Name
Address
City, State, Zip

Dear _____,

Our records from the Multiple Listing Service indicate that the listing on your property has expired. We would appreciate having the opportunity to discuss this property with you if you still desire to sell.

DO IT NOW REALTY is number one in real estate. I have the good fortune of being the number one associate in the firm both in income and closed volume. A brief out line of some of my credentials and qualifications follow.
• Number one in income for 1990
• Number one in closed volume for 1990
• Million Dollar Club (10 selected from 1,000)
• Number one in company every year in business
• Multimillion dollar sales every year in business
• Broker's license
• G.R.I. Designation (Graduate, Realtors Institute)
• C.R.S. Designation (Certified Residential Specialist
• Ohio State College Graduate

The individual sales associate can have a dramatic effect on the successful marketing of your real estate. Unlike most other professions, it costs no more to use the very best real estate agent you can find with a proven track record. Using a highly qualified agent to market your property will actually save you money and time.

Please review my qualifications and our company's standing in the community. We would be very pleased to arrange a personal consultation to discuss this property or any other real estate needs you may have. Please call me so that we can arrange a meeting to discuss how we can be of service to you.

Sincerely,

PROSPECTING EXPIRED LISTING

Date

Name
Address
City, State, Zip

Dear _____,

I see by our computer print-out that your listing agreement with DO IT NOW REALTY for the sale of your home has expired. I tried to contract you personally by phone, but was unable to reach you.

I would very much like to meet with you and tell you about our company and myself, and how we market and sell homes.

If you are still interested in selling your home, please contact me. The market has never been better for selling than now!

Sincerely,

Date

Name
Address
City, State, Zip

Dear _____,

It has come to my attention that the listing has just
expired on your property. If you still have an
interest in selling your property and have not yet
re-listed with another real estate broker, I'd like to
talk with you.

I'm the one who gets the job done if this property
is sale-able, and I believe it is.

How can I do what others have tried and failed?
Because I understand my job. We need to create a
demand for your property.

I've got a marketing strategy, and I need only to see
the property to be able to prepare it. Once you've
reviewed it, if you decide not to sell your property
then you'll know what went wrong. If you want to
re-list it, then you'll know where I'm coming from.
Either way, you won't make the same mistake
twice. I'll be contacting you directly.

Sincerely,

Date

Name
Address
City, State, Zip

Dear _____,

I noticed a couple months ago that the listing agreement on your property expired and you have not attempted to sell your home since that time.

You should be aware, however, that the market is constantly changing, as does people's circumstances. I believe that if you've reconsidered putting your house back on the market there is a possibility that your property could sell now, even though just a few short months ago your goal wasn't realized.

There are a couple important things to remember that never change when it comes to selling a property.

Pricing is crucial. You need to be careful not to price too high or too low. If it's too high you can have problems with appraising. If it's too low, there's the possibility that everyone will think that there is a problem with the property.

Make it easy, not hard, to buy. Realize that there is competition out there. You need to act like a buyer and not a seller.

If you need results, then you and I should talk. I can show you exactly what you're up against and what you can expect. I'll be in contact with you soon to see if we can get together.

Sincerely,

PROSPECTING EXPIRED LISTING

Date

Name
Address
City, State, Zip

Dear _____,

It is to my knowledge that your property (listing) has expired. I would like the opportunity to meet with you and talk about how our marketing efforts can sell your home.

DO IT NOW REALTY offers many services which are not available through any other firm. These services include a marketing plan, a market analysis and our national relocation service.

Accompanied is a brochure on DO IT NOW REALTY and many more services we provide. I will follow up this letter with a phone call should you have any further questions.

Thank You,

Date

Name
Address
City, State, Zip

Dear _____,

Our records indicate that your home has expired from the Multiple Listing Service. There are several reasons why a property does not sell. I specialize in solving the problems and getting action.

I would like the opportunity to meet with you and show you how my marketing plan can quickly sell your home. If you choose not to allow me to market your home, you may still use my successful plan. It will still be helpful to you should you decide to sell the property yourself.

I will be calling your number in a couple of days to schedule an appointment. If your number is not listed, I will pay you a personal visit, because I am dedicated to providing excellent service. If you are anxious to get your home sold as soon as possible, feel free to call my office and ask for me. Someone will be available to take your call, and I will get back to you immediately.

Sincerely,

P.S. Please keep in mind, I put my promises in writing.

PROSPECTING EXPIRED (RENTAL PROPERTY)

Date

Name
Address
City, State, Zip

Dear _____,

I understand that your property was for sale, but
the listing agreement expired before it sold. If you
still have an interest in selling your home and have
not yet re-listed your property with a real estate
broker, I'd like to meet with you and show you why
the property did not sell, and let you know what
you need to do about it from here on.

My job is solving problems and getting people
what they want. What I want to show you is what
we would do for you and possibly play a role in
achieving this.

I am aware this property is not your home. This
can affect the strategy when offering it for sale.
When you sell a second home or a rental, there is
a difference in the way this property needs to be
marketed.

I would very much like to meet with you and at
this time discover your intentions and goals. I'll
show you how I can help.

I'll be in touch in a couple days to set up an
appointment at your convenience.

Thank you,

Date   **SELLER COMMUNICATION**

Name
Address
City, State, Zip

Dear _____,

I am proud to be able to represent you in the sale of your property. I'd like to bring you up to date on what is currently being done to market your property.

1. Your home is listed in the Multiple Listing Service book and computer. Virtually every real estate sales person in the area gets this information on your property and will pass it on to the interested buyers they are currently working with.

2. All of the sales people in my company have the information on your property, and some of them will be touring your property so they can better market to their buyers. All of our company is working for you.

3. We are currently advertising your property in the local newspaper and local homes publication to get calls into our office on your property.

4. We have put a sign in your yard, which is one of the best means of bringing calls into our office on your property. The prospective buyer is already approving the exterior of the home as well as the neighborhood when they call in from a sign they have driven by.

5. We are currently in the process of scheduling an Open House for your property. Some of the other prospective buyers who have attended other Open Houses will be informed that your home will be open on Sunday, Dec. 17th.

If you have any questions, please feel free to call me.

Sincerely,

SELLER COMMUNICATION

Date

Name
Address
City, State, Zip

Dear _____,

It's time for another update. We've been working together for three months now to get your home sold. Let's take a look at what's been done so far and what you can expect in the near future.

We've adjusted the price which has brought more activity on your property. You may want to consider another adjustment in the event that our efforts linger on as they did in the past. That decision is yours, not mine.

Your home is listed in every issue of our Multiple Listing Service book and also in the computer. This is very important because it gets the information on your property to all of the professionals that are working with prospective buyers right now.

Your home has been advertised to bring calls into our office. Realize that even when your home is not advertised, and when we advertise a home that is in your home's price range, value or area, that calls are coming into our office and we tell them about your property as well.

I'll keep in touch with you on any progress I experience. Meanwhile, if you have any questions, please feel free to call me.

Sincerely,

Date

Name
Address
City, State, Zip

Dear _____,

We appreciate the opportunity to sell your house, and I'm sure Jane Smith, your listing representative, will get the job done.

Jane has already familiarized our staff with many features of your home, so you've got our whole team in your corner.

It's important to us that your home be convenient for showing. When as showings are necessary, we'll do our up most to give you reasonable advance notice.

If you have any questions call us at 555-5555. We're here to help . . . in more ways than one!

DO IT NOW REALTY can find that new home whether you're moving near or far.

Sincerely,

Sales Manager or Broker
DO IT NOW REALTY

SELLER COMMUNICATION

Date

Name
Address
City, State, Zip

Dear _____,

I wanted to thank you for the courtesy you extended
to our associates when they previewed your home.

It will be a pleasure marketing your property to our
prospective homebuyers. Please be assured that
our entire office will do our best to sell your home
as quickly as possible and for the best price.

Sincerely,

Date

Name
Address
City, State, Zip

Dear _____,

When we met the other evening I thanked you for allowing me to represent your property. I just wanted to recap some of the things we covered.

I feel honored that you have selected me in the marketing of your property, especially since I am one of many Realtors in the area that you could have chosen. I hope that the decision was made because of what I and DO IT NOW REALTY could offer you. The outstanding service and standards of DO IT NOW REALTY is the reason why I am with them and not any of the other companies in the area.

Here is the commitment I make to you. Now that you have put us in charge of your property, your priorities and needs will come first. We will do everything we can to give you the benefit of our experience and resources, which is why you selected us. Most importantly, we will always keep you abreast of the activity that we experience on your property. We will share the good news and the bad news unless you specify that you don't want to know, only when we get the job done. What we ask from you is that you value our input and advice, as we have your best interest at heart.

I'm looking forward to working with you and bringing you the kind of results that you expect.

Thanks again,

SELLER COMMUNICATION

Date

Name
Address
City, State, Zip

Dear _____,

It's been one month since your property has been on the market, and I'd like to recap the activity that has taken place.

Your property has been exposed to the Multiple Listing Service flyers have been distributed throughout the Board of Realtors to Realtors who are actively working with buyers, copies of your listing have been presented at our company sales meetings, and we have advertised your property in the local newspaper and homes publication.

Let me assure you that the activity that we have had on your property has been normal for this time of year and in you home's price range. I remind you that when we first started marketing your property, I shared with you that the average turn around time was 90 days. Hopefully, we can get action sooner than that, but at this point I want to make sure that you are not discouraged. The response we've been receiving has been favorable; however, we may need to take a look at the price at this time.

I'll be in touch in a couple of days with any developments that we may encounter before we sit down and further discuss the price.

Sincerely,

SELLER COMMUNICATION

Date

Name
Address
City, State, Zip

Dear _____,

Now that we've listed your property for sale, there are a few things that we discussed the other evening that we need to review. What we want to accomplish is to get your home sold as quickly as possible for the best price. Here are a few suggestions that will best-present your property.

a. Your home will have to appear in perfect condition. The dishes need done daily, closets and cupboards in neat order, beds made, etc. Things that you may not normally do each day but, under the circumstances, will need to be kept up with. The successful outcome will outweigh the hassle it may appear to be at the moment.

b. As we discussed, it is important that you are not present when a prospective buyer views your home. Hopefully, I can always reach you prior to the showing so you can arrange to be gone.

c. The exterior of your home is the first impression. Please make sure that lawn is kept up, the front door and garage doors are painted, any trim that needs touched up should be handled and shrubbery should be kept neatly trimmed. You never get a second chance at a first impression.

I'll keep you informed on how the sale of your property is progressing. Meanwhile, if you have any questions, please feel free to call.

Thank you,

SELLER COMMUNICATION

Date

Name
Address
City, State, Zip

Dear _____,

Now that you're planning to sell your home, here is a follow up to some of the reasons we discussed as to why your home needs to be priced realistically.

  a. Your home must be priced competitively with other homes on the market in your area and of similar market value. People will shop comparison and if your home is not competitive to what they are seeing, it will not sell.

  b. Overpriced homes will remain on the market for a long time, therefore, any buyer who is aware of this will think that there is something wrong with the property.

  c. An overpriced home will reduce the response that a Realtor will receive, thus reducing the chance of a sale.

  d. Other agents who are showing properties will tend to shy away from your property after they've shown it a few times and get unfavorable responses from their buyers.

  e. When you have an overpriced home, a buyer who is seriously looking for your type property and area will eventually settle on either another area or type property within their price range.

  f. If we cannot realistically price your home, I will not be able to give you the service that I want to because I will fail to get you the results that you want. The results being that you want to sell your home.

. . . continued

... continued

g. A lot of times failure to sell your home can result in your owning two homes, depending on when you purchase the one that you want prior to the sale of your property. This can cause you to double your current expenses, paying for and maintaining two homes.

Mr. & Mrs. Jones, homes that are priced right usually sell after a normal market exposure. Let's sit down again and take a look at the price you will want to ask for your home, keeping these possible obstacles in mind.

I'll be calling you in a day or so.

Thank You,

SELLER COMMUNICATION

Date

Name
Address
City, State, Zip

Dear _____,

Just a note to let you know that we appreciate your confidence in myself and DO IT NOW REALTY as we continue the marketing process of your home. Everyone in our office is working very hard to get your home sold. This is a buyer's market and this year was very frustrating for the seller and the real estate industry.

I am committed to my responsibility to you, Mr. & Mrs. Jones, and hope we will realize a success in the very near future.

Have a great day,

Date

Name
Address
City, State, Zip

Dear _____,

Now that we have listed your home for sale, I've listed a few tips that will show your home to its best advantage.

1. Keeping the lawn mowed, the flower beds weeded and the shrubs trimmed, gives the best first impression which will be a lasting one.

2. If you're planning to decorate your home, do it now. We don't want to tell the prospect how it will look, we want to show him how it looks!

3. Fix the little things that need done that you haven't had the time to do. Tighten the door handles, fix the dripping faucet, loosen any sticking drawers or cupboards, replace dim lightbulbs. Cleaning windows and unmarked walls will also help with the first impression on the interior.

4. Straighten out closets and cupboards. Clutter makes them appear smaller than what they are.

5. Clear the kitchen counters of any unnecessary items. Make sure the dishes are done up. This will help make your kitchen look bright.

6. Your rooms will appear larger when clear of toys and removed of any unnecessary items, especially the walkways.

7. Straighten up the bedrooms and keep the beds made up. Arrange it in the neatest and most spacious way possible.

. . . continued

. . . continued

When a prospective buyer is coming to view your house, don't plan to be home. Why?

a. The prospect may feel like an intruder if there are too many people present and will hurry through.

b. The potential buyer may feel uncomfortable and may not ask personal questions of importance to him/her if you are present.

c. They need to open the closets and cupboards. Many times they won't do this when you are present, again feeling like an intruder.

d. We need to answer their questions. We are better equipped to handle any objections, as well as any questions dealing with price, terms, possession, etc.

Thank you for your cooperation in these matters. I'm sure that if we work together, we will be able to make this a smooth transaction. Our goal is to sell your home for the best price and in the shortest time possible. That's what we both want.

If you should have any questions or concerns, please don't hesitate to call me.

Sincerely,

Date

Name
Address
City, State, Zip

Dear _____,

Thank you for giving me the opportunity to represent you in the sale of your home. I will do my best to sell your home in the shortest time possible.

Your home's appearance needs to be appealing. As we discussed, here's where you can help:

a. Get the little repairs done. There are things in your home that you don't notice but a potential buyer will. Dim lightbulbs need replaced, loose doorknobs should be tightened, etc.

b. Make sure your cupboards and closets are neat. Clutter makes them look small and unattractive. They will get opened.

c. Keep all clutter and toys out of the walkways throughout your house. This will also make your house look smaller. Keep dishes done and off the counters. Make the beds and keep your bedrooms looking attractive.

d. Keep the yard mowed and the shrubbery trimmed. The outside of your home will be the first impression.

I will always telephone you in advance before I bring a prospective buyer through your home. But sometimes there may be little time prior to the appointment, so it helps to do these things daily to avoid inconvenience to you when I need to bring someone over.

If you have any questions, feel free to call me.

Thank You,

SELLER COMMUNICATION

Date

Name
Address
City, State, Zip

Dear _____,

Please be assured that even though it's been four months since you've listed your property, we're still doing everything we can to get your property sold.

At this point there isn't anything that we could be doing any different to get your home sold any faster. We are committed to you until your goal is fulfilled. Our reputation in the community depends on satisfied customers. It is expensive for a realty firm to keep a house on the market for a long time! Costs are always going up, but we are still willing to do what it takes to get the job done for you.

I wanted your to know that even though you may get discouraged, we're not. We're going to keep on doing what's necessary until your home is sold and you're on your way to moving into your new home!

Sincerely,

SELLER/VENDOR HAVE AN OPEN HOUSE

Date

Name
Address
City, State, Zip

Dear _____,

We've had (2) Open Houses to date. I might add that they have been very successful. However, I know that your goal is to get the property sold. That's exactly what I have been working so hard to do.

I hope you understand why it is important that you are not present at these Open Houses. As I explained, a potential buyer never feels comfortable when the owner is present. He/She needs to feel free to be able to explore closed doors, closets and cabinets which is necessary for them when making a decision if the property is right for their needs. They also need to be able to ask questions which they might not ask when the owner is present. Remember, when a potential buyer goes through an Open House, they are actually going through a process of elimination.

I appreciate your understanding on this matter. I will be following up with each of the people that we know has previewed your home and I'll keep you informed of the situation.

Thank You,

Date

Name
Address
City, State, Zip

Dear _____.

Although I'd rather be writing you a letter of
congratulations, I still want to thank you for
allowing me to represent you in the marketing of
your property.

I know your original plans were to sell your home
and to be able to move on to a new home that
would better suit your needs. I'm just sorry that our
combined efforts couldn't pay off at this time. You
were a trouper as you went through many times of
adjustments which is very trying for anyone.

I would like you to accept my apology for whatever
didn't go right though this effort. I hope that if you
change your mind at some point in the future and
decide to try it again, that you consider letting me
represent you.

If you don't mind, I'd like to stay in contact with
you as I continue to work with buyers and sellers
in your area. Who knows what may develop?

Thank You,

Date

Name
Address
City, State, Zip

Dear _____,

It's time to sit down together again and go over a summary of all the activity that has taken place on your property.

1. We will review the prospects that have previewed your property.

2. Go over the updated market analysis on your home.

3. Talk about our future marketing strategy, such as advertising, telemarketing, direct mail and broker awareness.

You can expect to hear from me in a couple days to set a time that is convenient for all of us to get together. We can make plans together.

Sincerely,

LISTING ABOUT TO EXPIRE

Date

Name
Address
City, State, Zip

Dear _____,

I'm quite disappointed, as I know you are, that we have not yet been able to sell your former home. But being disappointed does not mean that we're discouraged. We request that you extend the listing to allow us to continue our efforts.

I think it's time we evaluate the situation. I don't believe the fact that your house is not sold is due to any lack of effort on the part of DO IT NOW REALTY. We have continued to advertise throughout the term of the listing. Also, your house has been exposed to many potential buyers through the members of our sales team and the Board of Realtors. I believe we must accept the fact that the asking price is too high.

You will recall that in my note to you in March, I mentioned that the market was slow for this price range property. A more realistic price could well be the answer, in that, many people who have viewed the house went on to buy similar properties at lower prices.

Enclosed is a Price Change and Extension form, and again, I have omitted the price with the hope that you will consider adjusting to $_____. Please give this matter your careful consideration and after deciding, please insert the price that you want us to ask, sign the agreement and return it in the enclosed self-addressed envelope as soon as possible.

In the meantime, be assured I am continuing my effort to do everything possible to obtain a speedy sale. I'll be in contact in a couple days.

Sincerely,

Date

Name
Address
City, State, Zip

Dear _____,

Thank you for talking with me yesterday. I realize that having your property on the market for four months without a sale can be very discouraging.

As you know, we have listed and sold many homes in your area and I'm sure we can give you the service you deserve.

When you are ready to put your home on the market again, I would be pleased to represent you. At you convenience, I would be happy to stop by and discuss the marketing process and to answer any questions you might have.

I've enclosed my business card. Just give me a call at my office or home if you have any questions.

I look forward to meeting you in the near future, and will be in touch with you soon.

Sincerely,

Date

Name
Address
City, State, Zip

Dear _____,

I wanted to communicate with you the activity that we have experienced on your property. We are still working very hard to get your home sold. As mentioned when we listed the property, this type of home does take time to sell.

I have three couples with whom I've been working with that are still considering your home. I am doing all I can to help one of them make the decision to purchase your property.

As your listing is about to expire, I feel it would be wise to allow myself and DO IT NOW REALTY to continue the process which we have started by re-listing with me. We are publishing an exclusive company magazine that will go to over 5,000 prospects, business acquaintances, friends and clients in your area and your property can be featured in this magazine.

I will call you in a couple days to let you know of any progress. In the meantime, please consider the possibility of re-listing your property with me so I can continue with what we have started.

Thank you,

PRICE ADJUSTMENT

Date

Name
Address
City, State, Zip

Dear _____,

Even though we are six months into your listing of your property, I'm not discouraged. I know at this point you are because you had hoped to be into your new home by now.

All of the Realtors in town know that your property is for sale, as well as all of the buyers they are working with. Yet, these buyers have bought other homes in your home's category.

Right now we need to completely re-position you in the marketplace. We obviously know that what we've done this past six months has not worked. There are a few changes that can be made, which will help in the marketing of your property.

While the decision is yours, I will make the suggestions that I feel will get you right back into the competition of the other homes in your area and price range.

I'll call you in a couple days to set up an appointment to go over the strategy we should aim for from this point on.

Thank You,

PRICE ADJUSTMENT

Date

Name
Address
City, State, Zip

Dear _____,

Your home has been on the market for some time now and unfortunately, the market is still in the same situation as it has been for the past few weeks.

We will be coming into a better season for selling. Take a look at what you've done and possibly what you can do. Put yourself in the shoes of a buyer, not a seller. Walk through you home and see what can be arranged or adjusted to make it attractive to the buyer as he/she comes through your home. Maybe the closet can be arranged to look larger, maybe a plant or an end table is out of place and makes your room look smaller. Is there clutter that can also make the rooms look smaller? Are the cupboards neat to look spacious?

If you're wondering at this time if it was a good idea to put it on the market, it is. The reasons you wanted to sell in the first place haven't changed. Don't get discouraged. There will be a buyer out there for your property.

We're continuing our marketing strategies of your property. However, maybe at this time it is also a good idea to take a look at your price. Is it comparable to the other homes in your home's price range and value? If those homes have sold and yours hasn't, that's probably why.

I'll call you in a few days and we'll sit down and go over our future strategies.

Thank you,

Date

Name
Address
City, State, Zip

Dear _____,

Your property has been on the market for six weeks now and it's a good time to re-assess the facts on activity.

There has been activity on your home, but each time the buyer passed yours up and purchased another one similar. As far as we can tell it's been because of the price. Every home that has been bought similar to the size and value of yours has been priced a little more competitively. Realize, I want you to get every dollar you can for your property, but it is time to take a look at what's been working and what's not been working in the marketing of your home.

I'll be in touch shortly to discuss this with you what steps we need to take to get us closer to our goal of getting your home sold.

Sincerely,

PRICE ADJUSTMENT

Date

Name
Address
City, State, Zip

Dear _____,

Your home has been on the market for some time now. It's not that we haven't had any activity, because we have, but I'd like to go over with you some steps that we need to make sure that we are taking. You need to put yourself in the shoes of a buyer and not a seller. We never know where the buyer will come from, so we need to make sure that all of these areas are covered at all times, just in case. My suggestion is that if you see anything here that you are not doing, let's start doing it because it can bring you that much closer to a sale.

a. Look at the price of the property and the price of other properties in your area.

b. Be willing to consider any offer at all times. You will have the final decision, but sometimes after re-assessing your area and similar properties in your area, the price may be more fair than you think.

c. Any recommended improvements that need done, should be done in a neutral color.

d. Please plan not to be home when a prospective buyer comes with a Realtor to see the home.

e. Allow a Realtor to show the property either with or without an appointment. I know this is inconvenient, but so is having a listing on the market for 6 months or more. If you are following the tips we went over when we first listed the

. . . continued

... continued

property, it shouldn't be too much of an inconvenience. The dishes should be done, the beds should be made, the cupboards and closets should be neat.

d. Make sure all rooms are free of clutter. Clutter, clothes, toys and excessive furniture will make the rooms look smaller.

e. Look at the house from the exterior. The exterior is where the buyer will get the first impressions and you never get a second chance at a first impression. Would the exterior of the home draw me inside?

Remember I am on your side. I work on commission and want to be able to get you the best price for your home, as well as get your home sold in the fastest time possible. Any recommendations I give you are in both of our interest.

I'll be in touch in a few days to see if there is anything we can do better to speed up the sale of your home so you can move with ease into your new home.

Thank You,

PRICE ADJUSTMENT

Date

Name
Address
City, State, Zip

Dear _____,

We've had your property listed now for four months. In discussions on your property with other sales associates they're telling me what I've suspected all along. There is obviously still a problem that we have not corrected that is keeping your property from selling.

Let me be candid with you about the price. For example if you know that your home would really sell for $95,000, but are asking $115,000 and think you'll see what happens, that's understandable. I want, as you do, to get the best price for your home. However, your home sits on the market with no promising activity, while you're still making your house payments and not moving any closer to your goal. Actually the best thing you can do for yourself is to place your home in a competitive price range with others that are on the market in your price range and area.

Anytime you have a problem or questions, please call me. But please call me and not a well meaning friend who does not have the experience of what we do for a living.

I'll be in touch.

Sincerely,

Date

Name
Address
City, State, Zip

Dear _____,

You and I know that your home has been on the market longer than what you ever hoped for. Certainly, with this in mind we need to realize that it will still be on the market longer in the existing circumstances.

We lost some valuable time in the beginning with not being able to make some important changes that needed made. The first stage is always important because that's when other real estate associates make their decision whether they will be able to place one of their buyers in your property. Even though we made changes later on, the impression can always be that the owner is desperate to sell. The problem is the owner that doesn't make the changes. Then their impression is that it will never sell.

Keep in mind that my job is to help you win and to help you not take so long to realize that win.

If you're feeling a sense of push because of your deadline to get into your new home, let me know and we can look at the terms you agreed on and maybe make a change that will make the difference.

Sincerely,

PRICE ADJUSTMENT

Date

Name
Address
City, State, Zip

Dear _____,

Your home has been on the market for quite some time now, but I'm not discouraged, because I believe that it will sell. If you wait long enough, anything will sell. We did get a late start on making the adjustments that needed made, but I feel we're on the right track now.

However, if you're not prepared to continue to wait, you might want to look at any other changes we can make that would improve your chances of selling faster, such as the terms of the sale. Certainly market changes will effect the sale of you home, but if you're more than ready, as I suspect you are by now, we will have to act upon the terms and possibly the conditions of the property to get the job done in a more timely manner.

We need to look again at the other homes in your area and price range and see what changes have been made there to be sure we are competitive. We need to look at all of these properties through the eyes of a buyer and not as a seller. Possibly there is something more we can come up with that we missed before.

I'll be calling you in a couple days to set up a convenient time to sit down and discuss this.

Thank You,

PRICE ADJUSTMENT

Date

Name
Address
City, State, Zip

Dear _____,

We've been working on getting your home sold and at a price and terms that are pleasing to you. However, since you're trying to encourage someone to buy your home instead of another one on the market, we've got to look at the property in the eyes of the buyers and not as a seller. Realize that a lender will not lend more on a property than what is an acceptable lending practice.

It's been going for quite a while now with no results. Frankly, it's not working this way so we are going to have to look at some changes. This will need done now if you want to sell your home. The longer it takes, the harder it will be for you to get the best price.

Our goal is to be able to make all the necessary changes, and re-list your property before the agreement expires. What you don't want is to have to start all over again with a new Realtor. Be assured that we're doing all that is possible under the circumstances.
Think about what you may want to adjust in the listing agreement the next time around to be able to get the sale.

I'll call you in a couple days.

Thank You,

PRICE ADJUSTMENT

Date

Name
Address
City, State, Zip

Dear _____,

I'd like to share with you the progress of the sale of your Main St. property.

This home has been shown many times by myself as well as other sales associates from the area. I'd like to share with you the comments of the prospective buyers that have viewed this home.

*For the asking price, the home needs too much repair. It needs updated, the wallcoverings need replaced, the floor in the 1/2 bath on the 1st floor needs repair, and the basement steps need replaced.

Competitive pricing is so important. The house down the street has four bedrooms, is updated and is in better condition. This home sold last week for $5500 less than what you are asking for yours. In addition, the lot is larger.

Mr. Smith, I am telling you this because it is part of my responsibility to you. My suggestion is that we take another look at the price. Judging by the prices in the area of homes comparable to this one, we need to consider a reduction. We always try to secure the highest price possible, but the buyers are resisting it and purchasing other homes.

In addition, I think you should consider an extension on the listing agreement, as we are entering a more active real estate market at this time.

I'll be in touch in a couple days so we can sit down and discuss the possibilities.

Sincerely,

PRICE ADJUSTMENT

Date

Name
Address
City, State, Zip

Dear _____,

Although your home has been on the market for 60 days, we are headed into the peak season for real estate sales.

There are, however, a couple things that we will be up against when a property such as yours has been on the market this length of time. One, people will wonder if there is a problem with the property since it has not yet sold. Two, the assumption may be made that either the seller or the associate may be hard to work with and that's why the property hasn't closed yet.

We need to sit down and talk about our future strategy and this will also involve pricing. We don't want to wait too long to make any adjustments and miss the additional activity we can generate during this peak season.

I will be in touch with you in a couple days and make an appointment to sit down with you at your convenience. Of course, any advice I offer is only my advice. You have the final say.

Sincerely,

PRICE ADJUSTMENT

Date

Name
Address
City, State, Zip

Dear _____,

I want to keep you informed on the activity of your property on Main St. We have had moderate to average activity, but have had no further offers, which is not what we want to be experiencing at this time.

I have this suggestion, Mr. Jones, based on the comments of the people that have viewed this property.

We need to adjust the price by $4,000. Although I want to be able to obtain the highest possible price for you, we have not had a good response from the prospective buyers at the current price. Each buyer that we have worked with eventually purchased another home of equal price but with less work to be done on it to satisfy their wants and needs.

I have enclosed a market analysis sheet for your review. I really believe that if we reduce this price we will experience greater interested activity.

I know you're busy, but please contact me at your earliest convenience to discuss this matter.

Thank you,

Date

Name
Address
City, State, Zip

Dear _____,

Although I was hoping by now to be sending you an acceptable offer on your property, this is not the case.

I have checked into other properties in this area that are for sale in your home's price range. Three of the properties are basically the same style and condition of your home. One home has been listed $1,000 below the VA appraisal and has been on the market for 1 1/2 years. The other was on the market for the same price as yours, but the sellers ended up backing out. Understand at this time that the appraisal and market price are not one in the same. Homes are being listed and selling below the appraisals.

Mr. & Mrs. Smith, I really feel that the market value of your home is about $3,000 below what you are asking at this time and I think you should seriously consider this reduction. We are getting low offers on your home because I believe that is the market you are in. Of course, you want this home to sell so you can move on to your purchase of your new home and I think reducing will speed things along. The longer a home sits for sale, the harder it will be to sell. Buyers that are aware of this will begin to think something is wrong with it; therefore, eliminating it as they pursue their search for a home. I feel that with this reduction, we will be able to get a purchase close to the new listing price.

I'd appreciate hearing your comments, and would like to sit down with you to discuss this.

Thank You,

COMMUNICATION ON MARKETING

Date

Name
Address
City, State, Zip

Dear _____,

The term of your Listing Agreement is about to expire, and I think it's necessary that we sit down and see where we are. I need to know where you stand at this point and whether you want to continue to sell your home. If you do, we need to deal with where you need to go from here to be able to get your home sold.

There are two questions that we need to ask ourselves as to why your home hasn't sold. Number one: Have I, as your Marketing Salesperson, in any way prevented you from selling your property? Have I not communicated with you what needs to be done to be competitive in the market? Number two: Are the terms and conditions such that it has kept you from getting an accept-able offer?

We need to take a look at the past months' activities. I have had other listings since I've acquired yours, that have sold. Why? Frankly, I think you need to make some definite decisions about what to do to remove the barriers that are keeping your home from selling.

Hopefully, between all of us we can come up with some solutions that will satisfy you. We have both a lot of time and money invested in the marketing of your property, and I want your home to sell just as much as you do. We just need to look at what we have to do to improve the your chances.

I'll be in touch in a couple of days.

Thank you,

Date

Name
Address
City, State, Zip

Dear _____,

Enclosed please find a copy of the ad(s) for your property which appeared in the following publications:

Sunday, Oct. 21, 1991 - Major Newspaper
Thursday, Oct. 18, 1991 - Local Newspaper
Oct. 11 - 24, 1991 - Area Homes Magazine

Advertising plays a major part in the marketing of your property through our company. If you have any comments or changes, please do not hesitate to call me.

Sincerely,

FOLLOW UP TO SHOWING

Date

Name
Address
City, State, Zip

Dear _____,

I wanted to follow up with you on the activity experienced on your property since we last spoke. We've had three more inquiries since the last offer I sent you.

On November 25 I thought we had the house sold. The husband was impressed with the home for the price you were asking, but the wife was not happy with the wall coverings. Even when I suggested what they might do to make it more appealing to her, she wasn't willing to go to that much trouble. One of the inquiries did not call back and the other purchased another home.

As you are aware, the listing is up on January 3rd. Of course, we would want to renew the listing agreement with you. I've enclosed the necessary forms for your signature.

Mr. & Mrs. Jones, please be assured that we have done everything possible to get your home sold. We've responded to all inquiries and shown your home to everyone that wanted to see it.

I thought you might be interested in some of the comments I've been hearing from the people that I, as well as other sales associates, have shown the house to.

• The price is too high
• The house needs updated
• There is too much repair work to be done
• The wall coverings are not updated

. . . continued

... continued

- The driveway needs gravel
- There is no air conditioning
- The kitchen needs updated

Please be assured that all comments weren't negative. These comments were positive:

- The size of the lot is attractive
- The lot is beautifully treed
- The rooms are nice and large
- Close to convenience but yet far enough away
- Nice school district
- Good potential

Mr. & Mrs. Jones, the house has been shown a total of twenty five times by myself and other associates. I believe the high interest rates along with the asking price is what is preventing the house from selling. Believe me, I'm not trying to make an excuse for why your home has not sold yet, but I think that I have done as good a job as anyone could have. However, should you decide that you still want to continue to sell, we should look at the price and that of the other homes that are for sale in the area, and make an adjustment so that your home is more competitive.

I look forward to hearing from you.

Sincerely,

FOLLOW UP TO LISTING PRESENTATION

Date

Name
Address
City, State, Zip

Dear _____,

Thank you for giving me the opportunity to present my services to you and Mrs. Jones concerning the sale of your home.

Again, I would like you to consider what DO IT NOW REALTY and myself have to offer you:

a. We have an office staff of over 50 sales associates that will be working on your behalf.

b. We offer you honesty, integrity and experience in real estate.

c. Our sales associates schedule showings at convenient hours.

d. We offer the services of our Multiple Listing Service.

e. We can arrange financing through a variety of places.

f. We offer you advice on what to do to make your home appealing to the prospective buyers.

g. We will show your property to only those who are qualified buyers.

h. We will advertise your property at our discretion to interest more buyers.

. . . continued

. . . continued

i. We will hold Open Houses to further generate activity on your property.

j. We strictly adhere to the Realtor's Code of Ethics.

Our office and our sales associates have an excellent reputation in our area. We pride ourselves on service and satisfied customers. This is what we built our business on. We'd like to add you to that list.

I will give you a call in a couple days to further discuss this. Again, I thank you for your time and consideration.

Sincerely,

FOLLOW UP TO LISTING PRESENTATION

Date

Name
Address
City, State, Zip

Dear _____,

I would like to thank you for giving me the opportunity to visit with you and discuss the selling of your home.

I want to assure you that should you decide to list with me and DO IT NOW REALTY, we will do everything we can to ensure a sale in as short of time as possible and for the best price we can.

If I can answer anymore questions, please don't hesitate to call. I'll look forward to hearing from you.

Sincerely,

Date

Name
Address
City, State, Zip

Dear _____,

Thank you very much for the time you spent discussing the possibility of DO IT NOW REALTY marketing your home.

There are specific facts which I feel you should consider when selecting a Realtor firm. I think it would be of interest to you to know that during 1990, DO IT NOW REALTY represented over (___) clients in either buying or selling their home. That figure represents many satisfied sellers as well as buyers. While we are very proud of this record, it did not happen by accident, rather by concentrated effort on our part to provide superior service. When choosing a Realtor, please take a moment to consider the following facts about DO IT NOW REALTY.

- We have the largest, most intensively trained, residential sales staff in the area.
- We have the largest advertising budget of any firm in our area.
- Our marketing program is geared to keep you informed of what is going on in our effort to sell your home.

I appreciate your reading this letter. I'll call you in a day or so to arrange an appointment so that I might answer any questions you may have.

Sincerely,

COMMUNICATION ON SELLER COMMERCIAL

Date

Name
Address
City, State, Zip

Dear _____,

We appreciate the opportunity to sell your business and I'm sure John Smith, your listing salesperson, will get the job done.

John has already familiarized our staff with your business so you have our whole team in your corner.

It is important to us that the marketing of your business be as convenient as possible. When such things as showings are necessary, we'll do our utmost to make sure they do not disrupt the daily operation of the business.

If you have any questions, whatsoever, call us at 555-5555. We're here to help . . . in more ways than one!

Sincerely,

Broker

Date

Name
Address
City, State, Zip

Dear _____,

DO IT NOW REALTY, in its ever continuing commitment to better serve our selling cliental, is proud to announce the publication of our DO IT NOW REALTY Commercial Investment Facts Sheets.

This Facts Sheet will be sent to hundreds of businesses, individuals, and professionals throughout various areas.

We have enclosed a copy for your review and thank you for the opportunity to serve your needs.

Thank You,

Date

Name
Address
City, State, Zip

Dear _____,

A few years ago we represented you in the sale of your home on 1234 Main St.

Now is the time to buy or sell a home. Interest rates are better than they have been for a long time. Should you be considering a move at this time, I would welcome the opportunity to represent you again.

I hope you were satisfied with my service on your last transaction, and I look forward to working with you again. If you should know of anyone looking to buy or sell a home, please keep me in mind. I've enclosed a couple business cards for your friends or relatives.

I offer a FREE Market Analysis with no obligation.

Sincerely,

FOLLOW UP TO BUYER

Date

Name
Address
City, State, Zip

Dear _____,

I appreciate the opportunity to be working with you. I work with a limited number of clients that are looking to purchase a home so that I can do my best to find the right home for you.

I will show you any home that you want to see, whether the home is listed by me or my company, or another firm.

If you come across an Open House that you would like to see, please let me know and I will arrange it. If you give your name to a sales associate showing the house, you will become his prospect. I would like you to continue to work with me. We are establishing, as we are touring homes, what your likes and dislikes are. I feel that I understand this and can do the job for you in researching the available homes that I think you might be interested in. Why start again with someone new?

If you have any questions at all, please feel free to call me anytime.

Sincerely,

Date

Name
Address
City, State, Zip

Dear _____,

Unfortunately we've been out several times looking at the homes available, and we've not been able to find that right home for you yet. I'm confident that the home you're looking for is out there.

I appreciate your not wanting to settle for less than what you want because I wouldn't want you to. We want satisfied customers, our reputation depends on it.

However, I do think you should re-analyze what you're looking for in your new home, some times when a person has looked at as many houses as you have, he/she may have a tendency to change his/her mind mid-stream.

I'm watching for homes that come new to the market in the area you're looking for, so if there's anything in particular you'd want different than what we'd discussed, please let me know. Otherwise, I'll be in contact with you with anything else I think you'd be interested in.

Don't give up hope. We'll have you in your new home soon.

Thank you,

FOLLOW UP TO BUYER

Date

Name
Address
City, State, Zip

Dear _____,

I'm sorry that the homes that we viewed today did not meet all of the requirements that you're looking for in your new home. What we did accomplish is that we found our more about what would make you and your family happy that we didn't discuss before.

Although there are more homes going on the market every day, I do want you to keep in mind that at the current time, the area and price range home that you're looking for is somewhat limited. If you can be patient, the right home will come up. If you're in more of a hurry, you may possibly make a decision that you may not be happy with in the long run. We at DO IT NOW REALTY pride ourselves on satisfied customers, and we don't want a hurried decision to make you unhappy.

We should take a look at some of the many means of financing available and possibly be able to place you in a home more affordable than what you thought you could afford when you originally gave me your price range.

Meanwhile, I'll be looking at the marketplace and hopefully be able to show you something more suitable next time, now that I understand more your needs.

I'll call you in a few days and let you know what I've come up with.

Sincerely,

Date

Name
Address
City, State, Zip

Dear _____,

Now that we've had a chance to view a few properties together, hopefully I understand what you want and you've got an idea of what's available in the area you want to live and the price range you're looking for. I'm as anxious as you are to find the right property.

I do want to mention, however, that the more properties you will see, the more confused you will get. One will have one thing you want and another will have something else. And next you'll be saying, "if only we could put this and this together!" Believe me, you're not alone.

I think it's time again to sit down and take a look at exactly what you're looking for. A lot of times after you've seen several properties your original wants and needs change. This is not uncommon. Many people say, "I want this in my new home", and "I want to live here", and we end up placing them somewhere else with different amenities than what they started out with.

I'll be in contact with you in a few days to discuss any changes you may have, and we can go from there.

Sincerely,

FOLLOW UP TO BUYER

Date

Name
Address
City, State, Zip

Dear _____,

I understand that you viewed the property I have listed at 1234 Main St.   Since this is not the only listing on the marketing in this area and price range, I appreciate that you took the time to see this home.

As I am constantly looking for comments from people like yourself who view this home, I would appreciate any input you would have that would help me in my continued marketing process of the home. I'd like your opinion on how this home compares to others, of the same interest, that you have been looking at.

If I can answer any additional questions that you might have about this property, please feel free to give me a call.

Sincerely,

Date

Name
Address
City, State, Zip

Dear _____,

Although you were not interested in the property
I showed you on _____. I
want to thank you for using my services.

Each time you see a property that you're not
satisfied with, I learn a little more about what
you're looking for. I will continue to look for the
right property for you. I, and certainly you, don't
want a property that you're not completely satisfied
with.

I'll be in contact with you in the next few days to
let you know what else is available that you might
be interested in.

Sincerely,

FOLLOW UP TO BUYER
Date

Name
Address
City, State, Zip

Dear _____,

Over the past few weeks we've seen several homes together. I appreciate your confidence in me.

There are a few factors I want you to consider since you're obviously anxious to make your move.

   a. With our Multiple Listing Service, we are exposed to every listing that is available in this area. If a property is for sale, we know about it. What does that mean for you? That you don't have to worry about looking, I'm doing that for you.
   b. We have weekly office meetings and tours of homes that are for sale in the area. That way we see first hand what is available and are better able to select properties for our buyers to view.
   c. Since we've been working together, I've gotten to know you and your family's needs. No one knows better what you are looking for, outside of yourselves, than I do.
   d. There is no guarantee that anything better than what you've seen will come along.

You might ask yourselves, have any of the properties we've seen come close to what we're looking for? Do we want to pass up an opportunity on a property that could suit our needs waiting for something else that may never come?

The decision is yours. I will keep looking. However, in view of the fact that the time is drawing near for you to move, you might want to reconsider some of the properties we've already seen, as at this time, they are the best suited to your needs.

I'll be in touch.

Sincerely,

Date

Name
Address
City, State, Zip

Dear _____,

It has now been (___) days since we've been working together and we've seen (___) properties that are available in the area.

Remember, that while I'll do anything and everything possible to find the property you're looking for, the decision is going to be yours. The "perfect" home does not exist. Even people who have built homes find that there is things that they would have done differently if had to do over.

There have been homes available for you to choose from and I have been actively looking for more.

I don't want you to make a decision on a property that you will be unhappy with; but at this point in time, I've shown you what's available. Also, many of the homes that I've shown you are no longer available. If there is a home that you are interested in, you need to make a decision based on the fact that there will be a buyer for that home. I just hope you choose before your choices are gone.

I'll be calling in a couple days to see where you want to go from here. Maybe, as is the case many times, you've changed your mind about what you want. If that's so, I need to know as I continue to search for a home that might be suitable for you.

Sincerely,

FOLLOW UP TO BUYER PHONE CALL

Date

Name
Address
City, State, Zip

Dear _____,

Thank you for your telephone call on the property located at _____.
I've enclosed a listing sheet that covers basic factors about the home. I've also enclosed information on some other properties that have similar amenities that you've expressed an interest in, as well as the area and price range you're looking for.

I'll be in touch in a couple days to set up a time that is convenient for you to view the property you called on, and also possibly to see some of the others I've enclosed.

Thank You,

FOLLOW UP TO BUYER PHONE CALL

Date

Name
Address
City, State, Zip

Dear _____,

Thank you for the opportunity to work together. We wanted to confirm with you what my goal and the goal of my company is as we begin our search for your new home.

1. We do everything. We want to help you make the best buy, in the most timely fashion possible.
2. We make the investment of time and energy all up front in the process of looking for a home.
3. We'll do all the searching for you. When we understand what you're looking for, we'll research the market, get the information on the property and make the appointments.
4. We take the time to meet with you and will go with you to view the property.
5. We keep aware of all the new properties that come on the market so that we're able to let you know when a property in your price range and area is available.
6. You, as a buyer, pay nothing. The commission comes from the seller when you choose to buy a property.

All we ask in return is that when you do decide to purchase a property, that you let us handle the transaction. I'm confident that we'll be able to find a property that will suit your needs.

I'll call you in a couple days so that we can set up an appointment in order to become familiar with what you are looking for and start searching for that right home for you.

Thank you again for the opportunity,

CONFIRMING APPOINTMENT

Date

Name
Address
City, State, Zip

Dear _____,

This is to confirm the appointment we have to meet each other on (Date) at (Time). I'm looking forward to working with you to meet you and your families needs.

When we sit down, I will be getting to know you and your family. What I want to accomplish is to be able to place you in a new home within the budget that you're working with and at the same time be able to get you what you expect out of this new home.

I work with Realtors throughout the area who have many many homes available. What we need to determine is what you're looking for, what you can afford, and what area you prefer to live in. I'm confident that what you're looking for will be out there.

I look forward to getting together with you.

Sincerely,

Date

Name
Address
City, State, Zip

Dear _____,

If you are considering buying a home, talk with me! I'll show you how I can make your homebuying experience easier and more convenient for you!

DO IT NOW REALTY and I can prove that we have one of the most advanced real estate systems in the market today. That means I can give you the competitive edge so you can find the home you want fast. Then I'll make sure your real estate transaction is a smooth process for you, from beginning to end.

Put me to the test. Let me show you how I can help you better than any other broker around and how my tools mean less hassles and fast, more efficient results for you!

I'll be in touch. In the meantime, if I can help in any way, don't hesitate to call.

Sincerely,

PROSPECTING FOR BUYER

Date

Name
Address
City, State, Zip

Dear _____,

Traditionally, spring is the time of year when homes come on the market. It's only February, and we are finding a large number of homes for you to view.

If you are considering buying property, you couldn't find a better time than now. The selection is good and the interest rates remain "affordable".

At DO IT NOW REALTY, we have what you need to find the right home for you and your family.

Work with me, I'll get the job done quickly, easily and hassle-free.

Sincerely,

Date

Name
Address
City, State, Zip

Dear _____,

If you want to find a home that matches your needs, call me!

I can enter your buyer specifications into our computerized system and instantly know which homes meet your qualifications.

It doesn't stop there. Once I've found the right home for you, I will track and guide your escrow process to insure that your sale closes with minimum hassle.

Call me. I can help you find that special property in the fastest, most effective way possible with services and systems available through DO IT NOW REALTY.

Sincerely,

Date

Name
Address
City, State, Zip

Dear _____.

Since you have been advertising your home for sale, it might be a good time to think about the assistance that DO IT NOW REALTY could provide in the sale of your home.

There are many reasons for the consideration of our firm. Over 300 full-time, professional sales associates give your listing widespread exposure, and each has a strong personal incentive to sell your home. In 1990, the DO IT NOW REALTY team represented more than (_____) buyers and sellers in our area.

As a member of a national referral network, we are in touch with many brokers around the nation who keeps us informed of transferees moving into our area.

In 1990, my personal production was over (___) dollars in sales. For the past 10 years I have been active in the profession.

My number one goal is to sell my listings. May I list your home to help you obtain your goal? Remember, there is no substitute for experience.

Sincerely,

Date

Name
Address
City, State, Zip

Dear _____,

REAL ESTATE
VALUES
ARE SOARING!

YOUR
PHOTO
HERE

Call Jane Smith
For A Free

COMPUTER MARKET
ANALYSIS

on the value of your property

at
555-5555

Sincerely,

Date

Name
Address
City, State, Zip

Dear _____,

I just wanted to follow up with you and let you
know I'm still in the real estate business.

If you or anyone you know are thinking of buying
or selling a home, or possibly even relocating into
or out of the area, please keep me in mind!

Sincerely,

Date

Name
Address
City, State, Zip

Dear _____,

If you're currently looking to buy a home, you already know it's an extremely competitive marketplace today. That's why DO IT NOW REALTY and I are ready to help, offering you that extra edge to find and help you buy the home you want . . . . quickly.

I can instantly pre-qualify you for a loan so you know how much money you can spend, and what price range of homes you should be looking for. You won't believe how much time and effort can be saved this way!

And when it comes time to open escrow, I'll make sure you know exactly what's transpiring, every step of the way!

There's more . . . much much more!

Call me today. I can help you in ways other broker's can't to find that dream home, and find it fast.

Sincerely,

Date

Name
Address
City, State, Zip

Dear _____,

I'm proud to announce that I've been able to secure a position with one of the top real estate companies in the area, thanks to special people like you. Because of my large influential clientele, DO IT NOW REALTY even considered me for association with their firm.

Because I am now with DO IT NOW REALTY, I will now be able to offer even a greater range of services than I had been able to offer to you before.

My new address is 1234 Main St., Canton, Ohio 44718 and the phone number is 555-5555. I've enclosed a business card for your convenience.

As always, if you need any of my services, please feel free to call me or stop in the office at any time.

Sincerely,

Date

Name
Address
City, State, Zip

Dear _____,

It gives me great pleasure to announce that I am now associated with DO IT NOW REALTY.

Having lived in this area all of my life, I am well aware of the many advantages of our neighborhood. We have a most desirable community, with easy access to freeways, proximity to a wide variety of shopping centers, and a civic-minded community association.

If there is any way that I can be of assistance to you and your family in fulfilling your real estate requirements, please feel free to call me. I look forward to being of service.

Sincerely,

Date

Name
Address
City, State, Zip

Dear _____,

As a resident of this neighborhood, it is my good fortune to have many friends in this area and to be well-acquainted with the neighborhood and its properties.

If your family is contemplating a move, I would appreciate the opportunity to discuss with you the services DO IT NOW REALTY has to offer. I might be of assistance in explaining current buying and selling trends, methods of financing, or in helping you determine the current market value of your home.

Take a moment and give me a call for more detailed information about a proven program to market your home.

I look forward to the opportunity to be of service to you.

Sincerely,

PROMOTE YOURSELF

Date

Name
Address
City, State, Zip

Dear _____,

Recently I wrote you about the Main St. home which I listed at 417 Main St. for $990,000.

I have already sold and closed this property and in doing so have set a record for the highest sales price obtained for a Canton home.

Call and let me put that same knowledge and expertise, that has made me a consistent multi-million dollar producer for the past ten years, to work for you!

Sincerely,

Date

Name
Address
City, State, Zip

Dear _____,

I'd like to take this opportunity to introduce myself
My name is Jane Smith, and I am a newly licensed
salesperson with DO IT NOW REALTY.

My company is well-known in this area as one of
the outstanding real estate firms, and I'm happy to
advise you that I will be specializing in properties
in your area.

I'll be stopping by within the next two weeks to
become better acquainted.

Have a good day!

Sincerely

Date

Name
Address
City, State, Zip

Dear _____,

DO IT NOW REALTY is proud to announce that Jane Smith has joined our staff as a Real Estate Associate.

Jane has previously worked as a 5th grade teacher at Canton Elementary School and is dedicated to the community and its needs.

We feel that Jane will be an asset not only to DO IT NOW REALTY, but to the people of Canton, as she is enthusiastic about our area and the opportunity of helping us make it grow.

If you are looking to buy or sell a home, don't hesitate to give Jane a call. Here at DO IT NOW REALTY, buying or selling a home is a team effort!

Sincerely,

Broker

Date

Name
Address
City, State, Zip

Dear _____,

Guess who's back in Real Estate? That's right - I couldn't stay away.

I want to ask again for your trust and confidence in any of your important real estate matters.

I've dedicated myself to marketing our wonderful community to people like yourself who have my love and respect. I'm proud to be associated with DO IT NOW REALTY, which many people, myself included, believe is the finest real estate organization in our area.

If you have any real estate needs, don't hesitate to call me.

Sincerely,

YOUR
PHOTO
HERE

Date

Name
Address
City, State, Zip

Dear _____,

My business is dependent upon meeting new people each and every day. I'd like to get in touch with those families who have added a new member, received a promotion, or the single who is just tired of collecting rent-payment receipts. You might even know or hear of someone being transferred into or out of your area.

I have the qualifications to assist people in attaining their real estate goals. You can be assured that people you refer to me will receive the highest degree of professional and personalized service from me and my company.

Thank you for your assistance. . . I look forward to hearing from you.

Sincerely,

Date

Name
Address
City, State, Zip

Dear _____,

When it comes time to sell your home, how do you know you have the right company representing you in this sale? It's easy.

You need a step by step marketing plan of what is intended to be done. That's what I'd do.

Make sure that the price you are asking for your home is competitive to other homes that are for sale in your area and your home's price range. That's what I'd do.

You should know every cost involved in advance so you know what you'd net from the sale before you make the decision to sell. This will then show you what money you will have to work with when you purchase your next home. That's what I'd do.

If you're thinking of buying or selling take a look at what DO IT NOW REALTY and myself have to offer you. Then give me a call. That's what I'd do.

Sincerely,

Date

Name
Address
City, State, Zip

Dear _____,

As residents of Canton and the listing agents for this impressive home, we wanted you to be among the first to receive our marketing brochure.

If you or someone you know has an interest in this very special home, please call us a anytime for a private showing. Appointments required. Now offered at $250,000 the listing price has been reduced by $50,000. We feel at this price this distinctive home will sell quickly.

Choosing a real estate professional to handle one of your largest assets requires the same careful consideration as the choice of any other professional to serve your needs. We pride ourselves on our hard work, 20 years experience, and aggressive, innovative marketing.

Feel free to call us for a consultation of your real estate needs. Of course, this will be at no obligation to you. We can give you a personalized program to obtain the results you desire!

Sincerely,

Date

Name
Address
City, State, Zip

Dear _____,

It is my understanding that your current listing has expired. I would like the opportunity to talk with you about how DO IT NOW REALTY can sell your home.

We sell more homes in your area than any other company. When one firm sells as large a portion of the market as DO IT NOW REALTY does, it cannot be attributed to mere luck.

I believe you will find that we have many methods of selling your property which are not available through any other firm. These marketing techniques include our Market Analysis, Individualized Marketing Plan and Relocation Services.

Enclosed you will find a small brochure describing our company and the many services we can provide. If you have any questions, or if I can be of other assistance, please phone me at the office or evenings at my home 555-5555.

Sincerely,

PROMOTE COMPANY

Date

Name
Address
City, State, Zip

Dear _____,

If you or someone you know has been thinking of selling a home, now is the time to act. Sales in your area have been brisk over the last year, and there is a continued demand for homes in this area.

As experienced professionals, we can offer many programs to help market your home on a nationwide basis as well as on a local level.

We are in the "people business" to serve your real estate needs on a personal level and we want to help.

For answers to your real estate questions, please feel free to give us a call anytime either at home _____ or at the office at _____. If more convenient, use the enclosed card. Of course, there is no obligation. This is part of our service to the community.

Sincerely,

Date

Name
Address
City, State, Zip

Dear _____,

We know your home is your castle ... but ... when you decide to sell, please give us a call.

A partial list of our services are:

1. Prepare a market analysis to assist you in obtaining the best price in the shortest possible time.

2. Include your property with our advertising in the real estate publications and/or newspaper.

3. Conduct a private mailing to the market whose needs best fit your offering.

4. Obtain additional exposure to your property by holding "Open House".

5. Provide you with a weekly report of our activities concerning your property.

We welcome an opportunity to put our 16 years experience to work for you. Please give us a call at 555-5555 for a free market analysis or if you have any questions. If your property is currently listed with another Realtor, this is not intended as a solicitation of that listing.

Sincerely,

PROMOTE COMPANY

Date

Name
Address
City, State, Zip

Dear _____,

There is always a market for prime residential property, and a core of hard working dedicated real estate professionals, to represent property owners in your area.

We know what you are looking for in commitment to your objectives. Call us for a team of full-time workers with the ability to screen the real buyers from curious lookers. Our talent for creative advertising, marketing, and financing are ready to go to work for you.

Good neighbors for twenty years, our office is located on _____.

Sincerely,

Date

Name
Address
City, State, Zip

Dear _____ _____,

It was a pleasure talking with you today about the sale of your home. If you decide to continue selling your home or if you choose to wait, you will eventually face the important decision of selecting a new real estate firm to represent you.

Our company, with its national recognition, attracts a tremendous number of out of state buyers. This many times expedites a sale where others have failed. We are the largest and one of the oldest real estate firms in the area with several offices strategically located and staffed with over 200 professional sales associates anxious to help.

We offer a national image and a local image through a well respected, old established firm name. I also work with a partner so you get two very concerned, professional agents working for you. We have enclosed our cards for your convenience with the hope you will give us a call so we can start working for you.

Sincerely,

PROMOTE COMPANY

Date

Name
Address
City, State, Zip

Dear _____,

It is with a great deal of pride that I introduce my firm, DO IT NOW REALTY, to my friends and neighbors. As a resident of the this neighborhood, it is my pleasure to know not only this neighborhood, but to be versed in our surrounding communities. I feel my knowledge of these areas can be of assistance in answering any questions regarding real estate transactions.

Perhaps selling or buying is the furthest thought from your mind at this time. However, should the need arise, for any one of the many reasons that prompts a decision for relocation, please contact DO IT NOW REALTY and me.

We have many years of professional experience in our various divisions, from Residential to Commercial to Relocation. We are members of the Multiple Listing Service and advertise extensively in newspapers and other media to reach both local and out-of-town buyers.

Enclosed is my business card for your reference, or if I can be of service at this time, please contact me at 555-5555.

Sincerely,

PROMOTE COMPANY

Date

Name
Address
City, State, Zip

Dear _____,

If you are considering marketing your home, here are some statistics I think you will be interested in! Since November 1, 1990, the following activity has taken place:

Total number of homes closed 41
Average selling price $280,000.00
Ratio of sales price to list price 93.3%
Percent sold for cash 50%
Percent sold during "Season" 52%

As you can see, NOW is the time to have your home listed for the best results in speed of sale and return on listed price. If you would like to discuss marketing your home or have questions regarding the current market value of your property, I will be glad to provide any answers I can or prepare a Comparative Market Analysis (CMA) of your home for your review.

Call me now at either of the following numbers to get the ball rolling on your home analysis!! Office: 555-5555 Eves :444-4444

Sincerely,

P.S. For those requesting a CMA between now and the 15th of Dec., the analysis will be FREE or CHARGE!

PROMOTE COMPANY

Date

Name
Address
City, State, Zip

Dear _____,

We at DO IT NOW REALTY pride ourselves on continued trusted service. A familiar name in our area, associated with integrity and quality service for over 10 years.

Some of the personal services that DO IT NOW REALTY and our Real Estate Associates provide are:
• National Relocation Service
• In House Mortgage Services
• Free Moving Program
• Specialized Advertising
• Free Community Meeting Area
• Personalized Service
• A Highly Aggressive Marketing Program
• Title Services
• A Homes Warranty Program for Buyer/Seller
• Special Senior Citizen Program

Come see us at our office and put ABC Realty's expertise to work for you.

Sincerely,

Broker

Date

Name
Address
City, State, Zip

Dear _____,

In the event that you're thinking of selling your home, I'd like you to take into consideration how our company handles the job.

As a seller, we represent YOU because you pay the brokerage fee at the successful closing. We work with YOU to get a fair price. Obviously, we want to get for you the highest sale price possible. Since we work on commission, the higher the price for you the better in turn we do. So if a buyer comes in at a low price, we're working for YOU.

When it comes to buying or selling property, you pay what it costs and will get what it's worth.

So if you or anyone you know, is looking to buy or sell a home, we hope you will keep us in mind. We'd like to be able to show you what we can do for you!

Sincerely,

PROMOTE YOUR LISTING

Date

Name
Address
City, State, Zip

Dear _____,

We just listed the property located at 1234 Main St. in Canton, Ohio. This home has 3 bedrooms, 3 baths and newly remodeled last year. It is being offered for $150,000.

Perhaps you know of someone who is looking to move into this area. We would be pleased to help them in any way.

Our office is very active in Akron as well as Canton. We have been located in the downtown area for the past twenty years; a convenient location to both Canton and Akron.

If you are thinking of selling, please contact us so we can discuss our marketing plan and what we can do for you.

Of course, if your property is currently listed with another Broker, please disregard this letter.

We are looking forward to hearing from you.

Sincerely,

Date

Name
Address
City, State, Zip

Dear _____,

We have now listed another fine property in Canton at 1234 Main St. As the listing agents, we wanted you to be among the first to know.

This professionally decorated home was renovated in 1989 and is beautiful in every detail. The new kitchen is light and bright and overlooks the lake. A gracious family room is newly tiled as is the living and dining rooms.

If you, or someone you know, would have an interest in this home on Main St., please call us at anytime for an appointment. We feel this home will sell quickly.

For a consultation of your real estate needs, feel free to call us at anytime. We pride ourselves on our 17 years experience, innovative marketing and hard work. We are never too busy for you! We can give you a personalized program to obtain the results you desire.

Sincerely,

P.S. If your property is currently listed with another Broker, it is not our intent to solicit that listing.

PROMOTE YOUR LISTING

Date

Name
Address
City, State, Zip

Dear _____,

As a homeowner in our neighborhood, I am concerned about real estate transactions in the neighborhood, and - as a Realtor - feel particularly qualified and available to assist them. DO IT NOW REALTY has successfully marketed the last two homes sold in the neighborhood, 1234 Main St. and my listing 1243 High St. Also this year, I found buyers for 1243 Cherry St. and my listing at 1234 Walnut St. Both new residents, Mr. & Mrs. John Smith and Mrs. & Mrs. Dan Jones formerly lived in the neighborhood. We welcome them back and applaud the stylish improvements they've made to their homes.

Now Mr. & Mrs. Jack Miller have selected me to market their home at 1956 Main St. Many of you know that this house was previously offered for sale. At my suggestion, selected updating has been done. In addition, we feel that the new price of $250,000 is realistic in today's market and will allow the purchaser to do further renovation. Do you know of anyone who would appreciate the amenities of the neighborhood and could take advantage of this good value?

This house will be open the first two Sundays in January, the 6th and the 13th, from 2 to 5 p.m. You and your friends are invited to come and see it on those dates, or if you prefer, call me for an appointment for a personal showing.

. . . Continued

. . . Continued

When you wish information on neighborhood sales or a market analysis on your home, please call me or return the enclosed Free Market Analysis. Many people looking for a home of certain size or architectural style have asked me to let them know if anything becomes available in our neighborhood.

Thank you for your attention. I look forward to seeing and serving you in the near future.

Sincerely,

Date

Name
Address
City, State, Zip

Dear _____,

I wanted to drop you a note to thank you for including my listing in your office tour the other day. I appreciate what you've done to make my listing more knowledgeable to your sales people, especially considering all the homes that are on the market.

I would be interested in any comments from any of the sales people regarding that listing or any suggestions that they may have for improvement. These comments help me to be able to make recommendations to my seller how we can better attract the right buyers.

Also, if any of your buyers might be interested in this property, please let me know.

I hope I can return the favor soon.

Sincerely,

THANK YOU TO REALTOR

Date

Name
Address
City, State, Zip

Dear _____,

I want you to know that even though the offer you presented on my listing on 1234 Main St. was not successful, I appreciate the time and effort you put forth in trying to put this transaction together.

Hopefully, the next time will fare better for both of us.

While I enjoyed working with you, certainly it won't be the last time we get the opportunity to work together.

Thanks again. If I have any buyer that might be interested in one of your properties, I'll certainly give you a call.

Good luck,

Date

Name
Address
City, State, Zip

Dear _____,

Thank you for showing my listing at 134 Main St. to your client. I'd be anxious to know if they showed any interest. I'd also be interested in any comments they have on the property, whether it be good or bad.

I've enclosed a list of other properties I currently have listed, as well as information on them. I believe that knowing what's available is the key to being able to best serve your buyers.

I'd like to be able to return the favor. If you'd let me know what you have listed, I'll see if I have any buyers that would be interested in seeing any of your properties. Although you can't guarantee what the buyers will be interested in, I'll certainly give it a shot.

Thanks again,

THANK YOU TO REALTOR

Date

Name
Address
City, State, Zip

Dear _____,

While you had a prospective buyer out-showing properties last week, you toured one of my listings. I appreciate that. You, like myself, make a point of seeing a lot of the listings that are available on the market so you know where the competition is. This then enables you to better serve your prospective buyers.

I am very much interested in the comments of your buyers and how they compare this home with the other homes they have previewed up to this point.

Any of these comments helps me with suggestions to the seller on what we need to improve upon to bring in the buyers that might be interested in their home.

If there is any interest in putting a transaction together, I'll do what I can to help you out on my end.

Meanwhile, I hope I can soon return the favor. Although we can't always predict what our buyers will be interested in, I'll be sure to keep your listings in mind.

Sincerely,

Date

Name
Address
City, State, Zip

Dear _____,

I'm really excited that we're getting one step closer to realizing our common goal. You, to place your buyers in a property, and me, to get my listing on 1234 Main St. sold. Of all the listings on the market, I thank you for remembering mine while you were viewing properties with Mr. & Mrs. Smith.

Hopefully, the rest will go like clockwork. I want you to know that I'm easy to work with; and as we're both anxious to see this deal close, we should stay in contact to make sure that all the bases get covered. We're too close now to let little things fall through the cracks.

Let's keep our fingers crossed that soon we'll both realize our common goal.

If you need anything, let me know, I'll get back with you promptly.

Sincerely,

THANK YOU TO REALTOR

Date

Name
Address
City, State, Zip

Dear _____,

What a successful week! Don't closings feel
great! Again, I want to thank you for remembering
my listing on 1234 Main St. I'm glad that the
Smiths found that it was what they were looking
for.

Everything went very smoothly, and mostly
because you knew just what to do and handled the
transaction very professionally.

It was great working with you and to be able attain
the goal we both set out for. Hopefully, we'll get
a chance to work together very soon.

Thanks again,

THANK YOU TO REALTOR

Date

Name
Address
City, State, Zip

Dear _____,

We did it! Everyone concerned met their goals!
The Joneses were happy with the price on their
property, the Smiths got the home they were
looking for, and you and I added two more
satisfied customers to our clientele list!

I want to compliment you on your professionalism
throughout the whole transaction. You were really
a pleasure to work with. You would really fit in at
our company. We have a terrific sales staff that
works very well together.

I'd love to sit down and talk to you about the
possibility of you joining our team. We can
always use quality people such as yourself. Give
it some thought.

Again, thanks for helping make this transaction
between us such a pleasant one. Hopefully, soon
we'll be able to work together again.

Sincerely,

Date

Name
Address
City, State, Zip

Dear _____,

Thank you for showing my listing on 134 Main St. the other day.

I wanted to bring you up to date on the property, as there have been some changes made you may not be aware of that may interest your buyers.

The price has been reduced $5,000.

New efforts have been made by the owner to help improve the interest on the property. First of all, they repaired the back yard fence for increased privacy. They have also put new carpeting in the living room, and added a new hot water tank.

With these changes made, possibly your client may show more interest in this property. Let me know if they want to see it again.

If you have had any current feedback or further interest on the part of your buyers, that we haven't already discussed, give me a call.

Thanks for your efforts.

Sincerely,

Date

Name
Address
City, State, Zip

Dear _____,

I have just sold the home of your friends Mr. &
Mrs. Jones. They have told me that you might also
be interested in making a move at this time and
asked that I contact you. They feel that I could
offer you the same quality service and success that
I was able to give to them.

I'll be contacting you in a few days to see when it
would be convenient for us to sit down and discuss
what your goals and needs are.

Sincerely,

ASKING FOR REFERRAL

Date

Name
Address
City, State, Zip

Dear _____,

Congratulations on your selection and purchase of your new home.

During the next few weeks we will be working together on the remaining details to maintain a smooth transaction. I would be happy to assist you and pick up any documents or signatures necessary to complete this transaction.

I'm sure that your friends and relatives are now aware of your new purchase. If you find anyone of these people interested in buying or selling, I would appreciate if you would give me a call. I would be glad to assist them with the same success we have experienced.

Thank you,

Date

Name
Address
City, State, Zip

Dear _____,

I want to thank you very much for recommending
DO IT NOW REALTY and me to Mr. & Mrs.
Jones. I'm sure that you already know that they
have purchased a lovely home through us at 1234
Main St. I'm confident that this home will be the
source of much happiness to the Joneses, and I'm
looking forward to keeping in touch with them.

Thanks again for the referral. Hope to see you on
the golf course as soon as the weather breaks.

Sincerely,

THANK YOU FOR REFERRAL

Date

Name
Address
City, State, Zip

Dear _____,

Thank you for referring Mr. & Mrs. Smith to me
and our firm.

We are currently working together to find the right
home for them. They are lovely people, and I
appreciate the opportunity to work with them.

DO IT NOW REALTY is providing the kind of
service you would want and the kind that Mr. &
Mrs. Smith deserve. Hopefully, I can reciprocate
in the future.

Sincerely,

Date

Name
Address
City, State, Zip

Dear _____,

I have built my business on referrals from satisfied clients such as yourself, and I thank you for the vote of confidence you show in me by trusting me to help your friends, Mr. & Mrs. Smith.

I have contacted them, and they are looking forward to enjoying the same success you have.

Again, thanks for letting me know that Mr. & Mrs. Smith will be making a move. I'm looking forward to working with them.

Sincerely,

THANK YOU FOR REFERRAL

Date

Name
Address
City, State, Zip

Dear _____,

Thank you for recommending Mr. & Mrs. Smith to DO IT NOW REALTY and me. We are working on a possible purchase right now!

Many thanks again for your referral. Hope to see you soon.

Sincerely,

Date

Name
Address
City, State, Zip

Dear _____,

Thank you, Mrs. Smith, for referring the Joneses
to me. I will do my best to assist them as we work
together in the sale of their home. I am confident
we will enjoy the same success that we had when
we worked together as a team on your property.

Sincerely,

THANK YOU TO PHONE CALL

Date

Name
Address
City, State, Zip

Dear _____,

Thank you, Mrs. Smith, for spending a few moments talking with me on the telephone this afternoon. I'll be stopping by to meet you within the next few weeks to see what we can work out together.

Sincerely,

THANK YOU TO PHONE CALL

Date

Name
Address
City, State, Zip

Dear _____,

Thank you for your phone call regarding the property we have listed at 1234 Main St.

In addition to this property, we have many more for sale. As members of the Multiple Listing Service, we have 3,000 other listings in the area. I can show you any of those homes as well. I'm sure several of these would interest you.

I'd like to be able to show you some of these homes. Please give me a call so we can get together again soon and review the homes in the area. When it comes to Real Estate, you need just one expert - DO IT NOW REALTY!

Sincerely,

Date

Name
Address
City, State, Zip

Dear _____,

Just a short note of appreciation for allowing me to place a DO IT NOW REALTY directional sign in your yard Sunday.

Incidentally, the open house results were very good in that an offer to purchase the property on Main St. was received.

If you, or anyone you know, has been thinking of making a move, now is a good time to give me a call. There were other people who viewed this particular property that expressed an interest in your neighborhood.

Call me for a free, no-obligation Market Analysis of your home.

Sincerely,

Date

Name
Address
City, State, Zip

Dear _____,

Just a short note of thanks for coming by my open house last Sunday at 1234 Main St.

Even though the home was not what you were looking for, I'm sure that we can find a home in the price range that suits your needs. We have listed many homes in this area, and I will keep in touch with you as they come on the market.

Sincerely,

THANK YOU OPEN HOUSE

Date

Name
Address
City, State, Zip

Dear _____,

Just a short note to thank you for stopping by my open house last Sunday at 1234 Main St.

I'm sorry that the home was not quite what you were looking for, but I'm sure that we can find a home in the price range that meets your needs. DO IT NOW REALTY lists many homes in this area, and I will keep you notified as they come on the market.

It was nice to meet you Sunday . . . I'll stay in touch.

Sincerely,

THANK YOU OPEN HOUSE

Date

Name
Address
City, State, Zip

Dear _____,

Thank you for letting me place the DO IT NOW
REALTY Open House directional sign in your
yard Sunday. By the way, the open house results
were very good, with a possible interested client.

If I can be of service to you in any real estate
related matter in the future, please call me.

Sincerely,

THANK YOU OPEN HOUSE

Date

Name
Address
City, State, Zip

Dear _____,

It was a pleasure meeting you at the open house on Sunday at 1234 Main St. Thank you for helping make it such a success.

If you have any interest in the home that you saw, or any within the area, I would be glad to answer any questions that you might have.

I would welcome the opportunity to sit down and talk with you and see what we might have available that would suit your requirements better.

Of course, there is no obligation. If I can help you, I will. If I can't, I'll be up front and tell you. Let me know if there is a convenient time when we can get together and discuss the possibilities.

Thank You,

Date

Name
Address
City, State, Zip

Dear _____,

Just a note to let you know that we appreciate your confidence in myself and DO IT NOW REALTY as we continue the marketing process of your home. Everyone at our office is working very hard to get your home sold. This is a buyer's market and this year was very frustrating for the seller and the real estate industry.

I am committed to my responsibility to you, Mr. & Mrs. Jones, and hope we will realize a success in the very near future.

Have a great day,

FOLLOW UP TO SELLER

Date

Name
Address
City, State, Zip

Dear _____,

Thank you for listing your house with DO IT
NOW REALTY. You can be assured that we will
do our very best to serve you.

We offer many unique services to both the seller
and the buyer. We have a Home Warranty program
that we will feel is an equitable one and would be
an attractive feature to a prospective purchaser.
However, this is your option and we acknowledge
that you can choose to decline this plan.

Again, thank you for listing with us. I'll be in
touch.

Sincerely,

Date

Name
Address
City, State, Zip

Dear _____,

Thank you for selecting DO IT NOW REALTY to assist you in selling your property. In our capacity as sales agents for your property, we promise to perform our services to the best of our ability in order to obtain the highest possible price for your property in the shortest period of time.

DO IT NOW REALTY has made the information on your property available to all other Realtors through the Multiple Listing Service in our area, and we will work in complete cooperation with them.

We believe it's important to keep clients informed each step of the way so there will be no surprises. As we begin advertising your property, you can be confident that we will keep you up to date by sending you a copy of the ad as it appears in various publications.

Once again, thank you for choosing DO IT NOW REALTY. We pledge to serve you completely and satisfactorily in every possible way during the entire period of offering, sale and closing.

Sincerely,

FOLLOW UP TO SELLER

Date

Name
Address
City, State, Zip

Dear _____,

Thank you for putting your trust in myself and my company by letting us represent you in the sale of your home. We are confident that the trust you have put in us will be returned to you and then some. We will work to give you the finest client service available.

I've enclosed some of the ideas we discussed that will make your home more saleable. Remember the goal is to get your home sold in the shortest time possible and for the best price!

I'll be in touch in a few days to find out how you're progressing and also to report on any activity I'm experiencing on your property.

Sincerely,

Date

Name
Address
City, State, Zip

Dear _____,

Thank you for listing your house with DO IT NOW REALTY. You can be assured that we will do our very best to serve you.

We offer many unique services to both the seller and the buyer. We have a Home Warranty program that we will feel is an equitable one and would be an attractive feature to a prospective purchaser. However, this is your option and we acknowledge that you can choose to decline this plan.

Again, thank you for listing with us. I'll be in touch.

Sincerely,

FOLLOW UP TO SELLER

Date

Name
Address
City, State, Zip

Dear _____,

I would like to thank you for the opportunity you have given me and my company, DO IT NOW REALTY, to represent the sale of your home.

We have a well-trained sales staff that will be making every effort possible to help in this sale. Before we call you to set up an appointment to show a potential buyer your home, we qualify them. We will advertise your home at our discretion. We handle the many responsibilities and details of the sale.

Be assured that I will do everything possible to be of service to you.

Thank you,

Date

Name
Address
City, State, Zip

Dear _____,

I would like to thank you for putting your
confidence in me to sell your home. I trust that
with collective efforts, we will realize a success.

When you list your property with myself and DO
IT NOW REALTY, you have engaged the expert
service, knowledge and experience of a trained
personnel who will ensure every effort to do a
good job for you.

Your cooperation in these efforts at the time of a
showing will also help to obtain the qualifed
interested buyer.

Should you have any questions at anytime, please
feel free to call me.

Sincerely,

Date

Name
Address
City, State, Zip

Dear _____,

Thank you for the opportunity of letting me represent you in the sale of your home.

I, from time to time, will be sending you comparables from the area. I like my clients to be aware of the marketplace and what we will be up against in the future as we begin the marketing process of your home.

Sincerely,

Date

Name
Address
City, State, Zip

Dear _____,

I'd like to thank you for listing your property with DO IT NOW REALTY and myself. My goal, as well as the goal of the other associates in the office, is to sell your home in the quickest time possible, for the best price and the least amount of hassles for you.

I've entered your home into our Multiple Listing Service. I've enclosed a copy of what was submitted to be put into the Multiple Listing Book. Other Real Estate professionals in the area will be using this MLS Book when working with their buyers. If you have any corrections on what I've sent you, please contact me.

Since I will need to qualify any potential buyer on your property, should you receive any phone calls or visitors as a result of our DO IT NOW REALTY "For Sale" sign in your lawn, it's best if you refer them to me. I will then arrange the showing.

If you should have any questions at any time, please don't hesitate to call on me.

Sincerely,

FOLLOW UP TO SELLER

Date

Name
Address
City, State, Zip

Dear _____,

Thank you for listing your home with DO IT NOW REALTY.

We appreciate your confidence and trust in our organization. Our entire staff will be working to sell your property over the next few months. I hope this letter will answer a few of your questions and concerns.

Your sign should be up within 10 days of when your home was listed. If you choose not to use a sign, I urge you to reconsider since a sign is our most effective direct advertising on your home.

When your home is listed with our Multiple Listing Service, it takes between 10-14 days for processing and at that time your home will appear in the Computerized MLS book.

Seeing your home advertised is probably your biggest concern. Let's take some time to go over that. Please note that our ads are designed to give the buyer limited information. This requires him to give us a call for more details and features of your home. If we give too much information and oversell your home, it helps the buyer eliminate your home and he won't call us. DO IT NOW REALTY has spent hundreds of thousands of dollars to research why buyers call, what they want in an ad and how to write an effective ad. We use these techniques and know that they work.

. . . continued

. . . continued

Your sales associate should be in touch with you every 14 days to give you an update on your home's progress. We'll give you feedback on showings, buyers comments and the advertising.

If you have comments favorable or unfavorable regarding our sales associate's handling of your home, please give me a call. I want you to be completely satisfied with our service and will handle any problem or complaint personally.

DO IT NOW REALTY leads the area in listings and sales and has a well earned reputation for honest business practices. We worked hard for that reputation and will continue to work hard to keep it.

Sincerely,

Broker
DO IT NOW REALTY

FOLLOW UP TO SELLER

Date

Name
Address
City, State, Zip

Dear _____,

Thank you for your confidence in letting me represent your home. Let me assure you that every effort will be made to obtain the best price for your property.

We at DO IT NOW REALTY take pride in our successful sales record. I am sure, with your cooperation, we will be successful in the sale of your property as well.

I am looking forward to a pleasant and successful relationship with you.

Sincerely,

Date

Name
Address
City, State, Zip

Dear _____,

Congratulations, Mr. & Mrs. Smith. I'm happy that Jane Doe was able to assist you in the sale of your home.

She really enjoyed working with you, and I wanted you to know that we appreciate having the opportunity to help you.

The success of our company, DO IT NOW REALTY, is based on being able to satisfy customers such as yourself. I do hope this has been a pleasant experience for you and that if at any time in the future you require the services of a real estate company, you call on us for assistance.

Sincerely,

Broker
DO IT NOW REALTY

THANK YOU TO SOLD

Date

Name
Address
City, State, Zip

Dear _____,

I'd like to thank you, Mr. & Mrs. Smith, for the cooperation you gave me during the selling of your property. I always try to give the best possible service before, during and after the sale, and I trust that you were satisfied.

I would appreciate any comments that you would have regarding this transaction. As our business is built on service, I always like to know if there are areas on which I can improve upon.

Even though your property is sold, please feel free to call me if you should have any questions at all regarding anything to do with real estate, as I will continue to be interested in you.

Good luck in your new home and thank you again.

Sincerely,

Date

Name
Address
City, State, Zip

Dear _____,

Congratulations . . . . and Thank You!

We realize how happy you must be to have sold your house. This will enable you to get on with your plans.

Thank you for giving us the job to sell it. We hope you were satisfied with our service and will recommend us to others.

In order to help facilitate your move, may we suggest you use the enclosed checklist which many have found to be very useful.

We're here to help, just give us a call.

Sincerely,

THANK YOU TO SOLD

Date

Name
Address
City, State, Zip

Dear _____,

Now that the closing of 1234 Main St. is completed, we have occasion again to thank you. To be able to service you again is a real pleasure. We pride ourselves on our ongoing service and appreciate the opportunity to have been a success with you again. Your repeat business implies a compliment to us in that we have been able to continue to satisfy you.

If there is anything we can do to be of assistance to you again in the future, or if you have any questions please feel free to call.

Sincerely,

Date

Name
Address
City, State, Zip

Dear _____,

Now that your property has sold and all the details
attended to, we would like to express our thanks
for the opportunity to have been of service to you.
Our greatest asset is your satisfaction and we hope
our service has met with your approval.

If, in the future, you require assistanc in the real
estate market, don't hesitate to call DO IT NOW
REALTY. We look forward to hearing from you
again.

Sincerely,

Date

Name
Address
City, State, Zip

Dear _____,

Hopefully now that you have moved, your life is
back to normal. I would like to thank both of you
for the opportunity to represent you in the
purchase of your new home and most thankful that
you selected DO IT NOW REALTY and myself
to assist you.

Should you have any future question or problem
related to your home or to real estate in general,
don't hesitate to give me a call.

Many happy memories in your new home.

Sincerely,

Date

Name
Address
City, State, Zip

Dear _____,

CONGRATULATIONS! The sale has closed and your property is sold!

I want to thank you for allowing me to represent you in the sale of your home. Even though you had to make a few adjustments that you hadn't originally planned on, those adjustments paid off in the long run. We met your goal and now you can get on with the move into your new home.

I'll be in touch with you from time to time to see how things are going and to see if I can be of any help to anyone you might know that would need the services of a Real Estate Professional. If you should have the need at some point in the future to make another move, I would look forward to being able to represent you at that time.

Please feel free to call me if there is anything I can do for you.

Again, congratulations and good luck in your new home.

Thank You,

THANK YOU TO SOLD

Date

Name
Address
City, State, Zip

Dear _____,

Hopefully, you're all moved in and life is almost back to normal. We would like to take this opportunity to thank you for letting us represent you in the purchase of your new home and most thankful you selected DO IT NOW REALTY to assist you.

Should you have any futher questions or problems related to your home or to real estate, don't hesitate to give us a call.

Many happy memories in your new home.

Sincerely,

Date

Name
Address
City, State, Zip

Dear _____,

Now that your home is sold and the last details
attended to, I want to express my appreciation for
the opportunity to have been of service. The good
will of my clients is my greatest asset, and I hope
my service has merited your long-term good will
and confidence.

Feel free to call me regarding any real estate
matter.

For allowing me to participate in this transaction,
and for your gracious cooperation, I thank you!

Sincerely,

THANK YOU TO SOLD

Date

Name
Address
City, State, Zip

Dear _____,

Now that your home is SOLD and all the details attended to, I want to express my thanks for the opportunity to have been of service. My greatest asset is your satisfaction, and I hope my service has met with your approval.

Feel free to call me regarding any of your future real estate needs.

Sincerely,

Date

Name
Address
City, State, Zip

Dear _____,

Now that you have moved and life is back to normal (hopefully), I would like to thank both of you for the opportunity to represent you in the purchase of your home. I am grateful for the confidence you placed in me and DO IT NOW REALTY.

Please keep in mind that my responsibilities extend far beyond the transfer of title. Any time you have a question or problem, don't hesitate to give me a call.

Thanks again. I hope 1234 Main St. brings your many years of happiness and pleasant memories.

Sincerely,

THANK YOU TO BUYER

Date

Name
Address
City, State, Zip

Dear _____,

Congratulations . . . . and Thank You!

I'm sure you'll enjoy your new home and your
many new friends and neighbors.

Thank you for buying through DO IT NOW
REALTY. We hope you were satisfied with our
service and will recommend us to others.

We're here to help . . . in more ways than one!

Sincerely,

Date

Name
Address
City, State, Zip

Dear _____,

We appreciated the opportunity to work with you
in the purchase of your new home.

May your life in your new home be a full and
happy one, and we wish you the best of luck.

Because your home is a most important part of
your life and of your family's, your happiness and
satisfaction is essential to our success.

Just because the papers have been signed, our
service does not stop. If you ever at anytime have
any questions or need advice or assistance, please
feel free to call me. I will always value the
opportunity of service as your Realtor.

Sincerely,

FOLLOW UP GENERAL

Date

Name
Address
City, State, Zip

Dear _____,

Thank you for talking with me yesterday. I realize
that you are not planning to buy or sell a home at
this time, but I would appreciate your calling me
personally if you do decide to make a change.

As you know, DO IT NOW REALTY has listed
and sold a great many homes in your area, and I am
confident that we can give you the personal service
and attention that you deserve.

One of the services we offer is a complimentary
market evaluation of your home. This evaluation
can be helpful even if you're   interested   in
determining if your homeowner's insurance is
adequate and, also, in determining your net worth.

I've enclosed two of my business cards. Just give
me a call at home or my office anytime that I can
be of assistance. Give one of my cards to a friend!

Sincerely,

Date

Name
Address
City, State, Zip

Dear _____,

Thank you for talking with me yesterday. I would be more than happy to stop by and give you a market evaluation on your property and to discuss the different ways that you can arrange to purchase another home.

I can also bring a Multiple Listing book and give you a chance to browse through it in order to see just what's on the market in the area you desire.

DO IT NOW REALTY has listed and sold many homes in your neighborhood, and I'm confident that we can give you the same personal attention and service you deserve.

I'll be in touch soon to arrange an evening appointment. In the meantime, feel free to call me at home or my office.

Sincerely,

THANK YOU GENERAL

Date

Name
Address
City, State, Zip

Dear _____,

Thank you Mr. & Mrs. Jones for allowing me to visit you today. I particularly enjoyed seeing your beautiful rose garden.

I'll be contacting you from time to time and would appreciate your giving me a call if you hear of anyone interested in buying or selling real estate.

Thanks again,

Date

Name
Address
City, State, Zip

Dear _____,

I noticed in today's press that you've been promoted to vice president, congratulations.

Now that you are moving up the corporate ladder, no doubt you'll be interested in moving up and into one of the two $500,000 homes we have for sale at DO IT NOW REALTY.

Seriously, Mr. Jones, we at DO IT NOW REALTY have a large inventory of many lovely homes priced realistically and within the price ranges that you might find interesting.

Of course, my ulterior motive in congratulating you is to sell you a house.

Enclosed are two of my business cards. One for you and one for a friend.

Good luck.

Sincerely,

CONGRATULATIONS

Date

Name
Address
City, State, Zip

Dear _____,

Congratulations! I saw in Sunday's paper that you were promoted and I mailed you an extra clipping. Did you receive it?

Very often as a person moves ahead, his housing needs change. I'm inquiring as to whether you may be considering a move in the near future. I'd very much like to be your "personal Realtor".

If you have any questions about real estate or the market, please feel free to call.

Sincerely,

Date

Name
Address
City, State, Zip

Dear _____,

The years have passed very quickly since you
purchased your home 5 years ago this month.

As I take this opportunity to extend Anniversary
Wishes, may this brief note remind you that my
assistance is ever-continuing.

For the part I played in bringing you this special
occasion - I thank you.

Best regards,

FOLLOW UP SELLER ANNIVERSARY

Date

Name
Address
City, State, Zip

Dear _____,

Did the date escape your notice - or do you recall moving into your home 7 years ago this month?

I hope the years have been pleasant and you are as enthused about your home as when you first moved in.

If there is any way I can assist you to ensure continued satisfaction, please do not hesitate to give me a call.

Sincerely,

FOLLOW UP SELLER ANNIVERSARY

Date

Name
Address
City, State, Zip

Dear _____,

It doesn't seem possible that it has been two years since we closed the transaction on your home . . . but it's a fact.

I'm certain you are aware that during the past two years, prices have continued to spiral due to increased construction costs. You can be assured your investment has been an excellent one because, more than anything else, your property's value has increased significantly.

If you would like a complimentary market Analysis (market value) of your home, don't hesitate to give me a call. I am looking forward to our friend and business relationships continuing in the years to come.

Thank You,

Date

Name
Address
City, State, Zip

Dear _____,

I wanted to take this opportunity to let you know that I hope you are enjoying your home. You have now owned this property for 2 years. The anniversary of the closing on your home is this week. I wish you continued happiness.

Even though you purchased this home, I still remain interested that you are satisfied. My service will always go beyond the signing of the contract.

If you should need any assistance or have any questions at anytime regarding real estate, don't hesitate to call me.

Sincerely,

Date

Name
Address
City, State, Zip

Dear _____,

Another new year is just a few short weeks ahead of us. It is a time to sit back and think about all the good things to be thankful for . . . like friends and associates such as you.

The business you've sent my way in the past year is especially appreciated. It's been my privilege to help your transferred employees and their families to settle in their new "home town".

I hope you and your family have a wonderful time together over the Holidays. To all of you, we send the hope that the coming year will be rewarding.

Best wishes,

Date

Name
Address
City, State, Zip

Dear _____,

During this holiday season, it is traditional to pause and extend a "thank you" for all the good fortune enjoyed during the past year.

This season gives me the opportunity to extend my appreciation to you for purchasing or buying your home through us. I enjoyed working with you.

To you and yours, warm wishes for a Happy Holiday Season and continued health and happiness through the New Year.

Best Wishes,

Date

Name
Address
City, State, Zip

Dear _____,

With the end of 1990, and the beginning of an exciting new year, I want to express my gratitude to the people I've had the pleasure of representing during the past year.

Last year was by far the best that I've had in real estate sales, and part of that success was due to your decision to do business with me and DO IT NOW REALTY.

The referrals from my clients and friends have been the single most important asset in my growth as a real estate broker. You can be assured that your loyalty is greatly appreciated.

My responsibilities extend far beyond the closing table. Please let me know whenever I can be of service to you. Thanks again.

Best Wishes,

THANKSGIVING

Date

Name
Address
City, State, Zip

Dear _____,

Another Thanksgiving and another opportunity for me to thank you and to wish you and yours a Happy Holiday Season.

At this time of the year, it's natural that we reflect upon those things that we appreciate. Remembering friends certainly has to be counted as one of the greatest of life's pleasures.

Best wishes for continued happiness this Season and throughout the New Year.

Sincerely,

Date

Name
Address
City, State, Zip

Dear _____,

Just wanted to take a minute to thank you for everything you did concerning the processing of John Smith's loan. In fact, all of the work regarding their property was far beyond the ordinary requirements of any mortgage company and broker.

Please extend my gratitude and appreciation to Jane Doe (your processor) and everyone at your mortgage company for all their assistance and cooperation.

Sincerely,

FOLLOW UP RELOCATION

Date

Name
Address
City, State, Zip

Dear _____,

It was such a pleasure meeting both of you. In the short time we spent together, I hope that in some way I helped you to make the decision to move to Canton, Ohio. We're very proud of our community and feel that you and your family would be very happy living here.

I am enclosing some copies of new listings, as well as several others that we did not have time to see firsthand. Maybe one of them will be of interest to you.

Our affiliation with the Multiple Listing Service makes it possible for me to show you almost any home, and I'm interested in helping you find the kind of home that you and your family would really enjoy.

Please let me hear from you as soon as you make your decision to move to Canton. In the meantime, if you have any questions, don't hesitate to call.

Sincerely,

We are pleased to announce
. . . that
Jane Smith
has joined our firm
of DO IT NOW REALTY
as
A Real Estate Professional
to help you with all of your
Real Estate needs.

NAME
ADDRESS
CITY, STATE, ZIP

THE STAFF AT
DO IT NOW REALTY

is pleased
to introduce
John Smith

as the newest Real Estate
Professional to join our team.
Should you have any
questions regarding Real
Estate, please give him a call.

NAME
ADDRESS
CITY, STATE, ZIP

You Are Cordially Invited
To Attend an Open House
from 2:00 p.m. to 5:00 p.m.
at 1234 Main St.
on Sunday, Dec, 22nd

Do you have a friend or relative
interested in buying a new home?
If so, please invite them to attend
our Open House as well.

NAME
ADDRESS
CITY, STATE, ZIP

YOU'RE INVITED!

We are having an
Open House
in your neighborhood
and we invite you to
preview this home.
WHEN: Sunday, Jan. 3rd
WHERE: 1234 Main St.
TIME: 2:00-4:00 p.m.

If anyone you know is interested
in buying or selling real estate,
please invite them to come along.

NAME
ADDRESS
CITY, STATE, ZIP

We have just listed the home at 1234 Main St.

We would be pleased to show you this home at your convenience.

If you have friends interested in moving into this neighborhood, please let them know about this property and ask them to contact us.

DO IT NOW REALTY
555-5555

NAME
ADDRESS
CITY, STATE, ZIP

Your New Neighbors Are
Mr. & Mrs. John Smith

They have just purchased the home at 1234 Main St.

We are certain you will enjoy them as neighbors. I am sure they would appreciate any courtesies you may extend in welcoming them into your neighborhood.

Jane Smith
DO IT NOW REALTY
555-5555

NAME
ADDRESS
CITY, STATE, ZIP

We have just sold another home in your area. We also have other buyers interested in your neighborhood. If you would like a market analysis of your property, please give me a call. I would be happy to show you what your home is worth.

Jane Smith
DO IT NOW REALTY
555-5555

NAME
ADDRESS
CITY, STATE, ZIP

Recently I conducted a showing of your home. Below is a report regarding my customer's reaction and comments

Date of Showing: _____
Adults: _____   Children: _____
Current residency:
_____ In town   _____ Out of town
Comments: _____
_____
_____

If you have any questions or comments, please feel free to call me.

Jane Smith
DO IT NOW REALTY
555-5555

NAME
ADDRESS
CITY, STATE, ZIP

Dear _____,

I just wanted to drop you a short note and let you know that I showed your home on Monday, Jan. 25th. I'll give you a call in a day or so to let you know how it's going. Meanwhile, let's keep our fingers crossed.

John Doe
DO IT NOW REALTY
555-5555

NAME
ADDRESS
CITY, STATE, ZIP

Thank you again for giving me the opportunity to list your property. My main purpose is to bring you the best price in a short period of time.

As I promised, you will receive from me an update every 30 days. I have your best interest in mind.

Please don't hesitate to call me anytime.

Jane Doe
DO IT NOW REALTY
555-5555

NAME
ADDRESS
CITY, STATE, ZIP

I just wanted to drop you a short note and let you know that I will be calling you in a couple days to go over with you the activity that we've experienced on your property.

I will also, at this time, offer some additional suggestions I have that might help in the sale of your home.

John Smith
DO IT NOW REALTY
555-5555

NAME
ADDRESS
CITY, STATE, ZIP

Most of my business depends on referrals from friends and past clients. If you know of anyone who may be interested in buying or selling a home, please tell them about me and then give me a call.

And if there is any way I can help you, please let me know.

Jane Smith
DO IT NOW REALTY
555-5555

NAME
ADDRESS
CITY, STATE, ZIP

As you may have noticed, there are numerous DO IT NOW REALTY For Sale signs in your neighborhood.

As a resident of this community myself, I would be very interested if you, or anyone you know of, is interested in moving into or out of the area. I can be of assistance. Please give me a call.

John Jones
DO IT NOW REALTY
555-5555

NAME
ADDRESS
CITY, STATE, ZIP

NOTE ASKING FOR REFERRAL

Date

Name
Address
City, State, Zip

Dear _____,

Just a note to say "hello"! If I can ever be of service to you, feel free to call me. If you or your friends have any questions on anything regarding real estate, don't hesitate to call me. I would certainly appreciate hearing from you. We are looking for buyers and sellers.

I've enclosed my business card for you to keep for you reference when you need to buy or sell your home.

Thank you,

Date

Name
Address
City, State, Zip

Dear _____,

I thank you for your confidence in me during the purchase of your new home. I appreciate being able to work with you.

If I can be of assistance to any of your friends or relatives, please don't hesitate to call.

Sincerely,

ABOUT THE AUTHOR

ERNIE BLOOD
Publisher, Author, Trainer
National & International Speaker

Ernie Blood may speak to more sales people than any other speaker in the Real Estate Industry. He was co-founder of Homes Guide of America. Today he is founder and President of Carmel Publishing - America's up and coming publisher of Real Es ate photo magazines! Ernie is recognized today as a leade. in sales training. His warm, sincere and enthusiastic platform style has endeared him to audiences everywhere. Ernie specializes in helping Real Estate sales people market themselves to the top. Ernie is the creator of the "I DARE YOU" Course©. He is author of five best sellers <u>The Pocket Ad Writer for Real Estate Professionals, The Pocket Prospecting Guide For Real Estate Professionals, the Pocket Library of Letters For Real Estate Professionals, The Pocket Call Conversion Guide For Real Estate Professionals, and The Pocket Selling & Closing Guide For Real Estate Professionals</u>. He has also produced Video and Audio Training Cassettes for Real Estate Salespeople and Managers. Ernie's experience as a top 10 salesman with a national company has allowed him a depth of experience unique to the real estate industry.

CARMEL PUBLISHING CO.
4501 Hills & Dales Road, N.W.
Canton, Ohio 44718
1-800-344-3834

~ ORDER FORM ~

Please send me the following **Pocket Guides** at $29.95 ea. plus S&H: $3.00 first book, 50¢ ea. add'l book. (Ohio residents add 5.25% sales tax).

#		#		# BOOKS	PRICE
#	Ad Writer(s)	#	Selling & Closing(s)	1	$29.95ea.
#	Prospecting(s)	#	Self Promo.&Mrkt(s)	2-4	$25.00ea.
#	Library of Letter(s)	#	Assistant Guide(s)	5 or more .	$22.00ea.
#	Call Conversion(s)	#	Internet Guide(s)		
#	Library of Letters II(s)	#	Property Management(s)		

Name _____
Company _____
Address _____
City _____ State _____ Zip _____
FOR CHARGE ORDERS: ☐ Visa ☐ MasterCard ☐ Amer. Express ☐ Discover
Card # _____ Exp. Date _____
Signature _____

Make checks payable to:
Call 1-800-344-3834
or Fax 330/478-9205

CARMEL PUBLISHING, INC.
4501 Hills & Dales Rd., N.W.
Canton, Ohio 44708

| QUANTITY |
| DISCOUNTS |
| AVAILABLE |